Standing Strong Through Life's Storms

ONE WOMAN'S STORY OF LOSS AND PERSEVERANCE

Donna M. Trickett

Donna Trickett

TRILOGY CHRISTIAN PUBLISHERS

TUSTIN, CA

Trilogy Christian Publishers
A Wholly Owned Subsidary of Trinity Broadcasting Network
2442 Michelle Drive
Tustin, CA 92780

Standing Strong Through Life's Storms

For information, address Trilogy Christian Publishing

Rights Department, 2442 Michelle Drive, Tustin, Ca 92780.

Trilogy Christian Publishing/ TBN and colophon are trademarks of Trinity Broadcasting Network.

For information about special discounts for bulk purchases, please contact Trilogy Christian Publishing.

Manufactured in the United States of America

Trilogy Disclaimer: The views and content expressed in this book are those of the author and may not necessarily reflect the views and doctrine of Trilogy Christian Publishing or the Trinity Broadcasting Network.

10 9 8 7 6 5 4 3 2 1

Library of Congress Cataloging-in-Publication Data is available.

ISBN 978-1-68556-605-0

ISBN 0978-1-68556-606-7 (ebook)

Dedication

This book is dedicated to the memory of my husband, Arthur Nelson Trickett, who shared fifty-three years of his life with me and worked alongside me through so many of our fears.

So be truly glad. There is wonderful joy ahead, even though you must endure many trials for a little while. These trials will show that your faith is genuine. It is being tested as fire tests and purifies gold—though your faith is far more precious than mere gold. So when your faith remains strong through many trials, it will bring you much praise and glory and honor on the day when Jesus Christ is revealed to the whole world.

(1 Peter 1:6–7 NLT)

Consider it pure joy, my brothers and sisters, whenever you face trials of many kinds, because you know that the testing of your faith produces perseverance.

(James 1:2–3 NIV)

Contents

Introduction

Whenever we face a new challenge or threat, we will either go through it, or we'll give up, and our fears will multiply in our minds. As Zig Ziglar put it, "Fear has two meanings: 'Forget everything and run' or 'Face everything and rise.' The choice is yours."[1]

I have experienced the paralysis that fear brings at various times in my life. Ninety-nine percent of the time, none of the things I feared materialized. But when your mind is gripped by fear, your brain ceases to function, your knees get weak, and you want to run to a secure place or person.

You may seek the encouragement of a friend or spouse, only to find that they are paralyzed by their fears, or they don't have the solution you need. Filling your life with distractions doesn't help because, sooner or later, you have to face reality, and the reality is that God has been there all along?

---

1 "Quote by Zig Ziglar," Goodreads, Inc., 2022, https://www.goodreads.com/quotes/976049-f-e-a-r-has-two-meanings-forget-everything-and-run-or-face.

You may say, "Well, if He was there, why didn't He take away the problem? How can God allow this pandemic to go on so long? Where is He when I'm suffering after the loss of a loved one or alone in the hospital? I can't see Him. I don't hear Him."

He's there. You just have to tune into His frequency, distance yourself from what is happening to you, and take a look at the bigger picture. It's interesting that this generation, including many of us from a generation that never heard of a cell phone when we were young, love to take selfies. We don't even care if the picture isn't that good, just as long as it has me in the picture.

If we are always thinking of me, then we are not tuned into God's frequency. Our prayers may not be answered because they are probably built on our selfish desires. That's not to say that we shouldn't pray for healing or the things we need but are we also including others in our prayers? And do we remember to thank God for what He has already done for us?

When I was in my thirties, with two little children to care for, I would often be stricken by a debilitating migraine that would last for most of my day. As I felt it coming on, I would prepare some sandwiches and activities for the children, so they wouldn't be neglected as I tried to find relief from my pounding pain.

Then, one day, as I was listening to the story of a young friend of mine, who was enduring many physical problems, emanating from her recently discovered brain tumor, which had been deemed inoperable, I heard her say that she had excruciating migraine headaches every day. When I related to her that I understood what that meant because I've had them multiple times each month, she said, with great compassion, "I am so sorry! I will pray for you every day." Wow, I didn't expect her to pray for me; all her prayers needed to be directed to her healing.

My heart ached for her as I listened to her story, but, as we often do, I forgot about our talk with all the activities we had on our calendar. Then, as I felt the familiar pre-migraine warning alarms go off in my body, beginning with nausea and then stiffness in the back of my neck, I began to pray. Only this time, I thought of my friend, Lynn.

Without once asking for God to spare me, I prayed for her. She was only twenty-six and required a wheelchair. Knowing she was probably in the throes of a migraine at that very moment, I prayed that God would spare her. "Please give her a pain-free day, Lord."

To my amazement, when I ended my prayer, I realized that my symptoms had disappeared. I had actually put myself aside and concentrated on someone else. God gave me what I needed without my even asking. Maybe I wasn't the center of the universe, after all. Maybe God wanted me to know that I needed to look beyond my selfie and become more deeply involved in other people's needs.

Those dreaded headaches opened my eyes to the fact that I could grow in my trials and not worry over them because God was in the trial with me. He was not causing the problem but allowing it to exist for my growth. I mean, let's face it, sometimes we bring on our problems by the kind of foods we eat or the lack of activity in our daily routines. Back then, I was addicted to caffeine in the form of coffee and colas, which probably was a very real contributor to my condition. While I wouldn't exactly say that I *rejoiced* in my trial, as James 1:2 states, I at least wasn't overwhelmed by it.

Jesus said, again and again, to "fear not." So, how do we accomplish that? This is where we need to develop a personal relationship with God. Your journey will be uniquely yours, perhaps inundated by more trials than I experienced, but with time, God will show you how to look beyond yourself and take on the attributes of our Savior. That's not to say that I have attained those attributes, *but God's not finished with me,* and I won't be fully mature until I am standing with Him in Glory.

While it's true that God is ultimately in control of everything... He still wants us to be free agents, to make our own decisions. He wants us to discover that His way is the most fulfilling way to live.

As a result, God teaches us to make wise decisions through His Word and the urgings of His Holy Spirit.

But the final decision is ours. And I promise you; God will keep giving you chances to rethink your bad choices. You will never stop learning and growing as long as you live with God at the controls of your life.

Maybe you think the trial you are in is too big for you. Not a problem. It simply means you've been humbled. In time, you will become stronger and grow stronger by passing the tests, or what we Christians refer to as our trials. I mean, how can you know if you are gaining courage and wisdom if you are never tested?

The more you gain Biblical knowledge and a mind that is tuned to God's will and not your own, you will hear from God throughout your day. Don't expect Him to thunder from Mt. Sinai, but He will speak to you through a strong urging or a gentle whisper. "Nuh, uh... don't watch that." Or "come on, take the time to make a meal for your friend's family while she's in the hospital."

For weeks, I felt the urge to write this book. I had already written four other books about what I learned from the loss of our daughter and my mother in the throes of Alzheimer's, but with all the fears, anger, confusion, and misunderstandings that have erupted since 2020, I knew I had to write something. Something that might help to dispel the fears of so many people today, something that God had taught me over the last seventy-nine years of my life.

Subsequently, here is the story of my life's journey that keeps pulling me further and further away from fear, even though fear is embedded in each of my narratives. Each chapter tells of the fears I had managed to survive and even step beyond. I sincerely hope they will help you to conquer your fears.

CHAPTER 1

Where Does Fear Come From?

For God has not given us a spirit of fear, but of power and of love and of a sound mind.

(2 Timothy 1:7 NKJV)

Franklin D. Roosevelt had just been elected president, in 1932, in the very depth of the Great Depression. And yet, this is what he said in his inaugural address, "... the only thing we have to fear is fear itself."[2]

---

2 "Quote by Franklin D. Roosevelt," BrainyQuote, 2022, https://www. brainyquote.com/quotes/franklin_d_roosevelt_109480.

This was a man who had been very robust and healthy, as well as financially endowed, and was enjoying his wife, Eleonor, and their six children, when, at the age of thirty-nine, he was stricken with polio.[3] It left him wheelchair-bound for the rest of his life. All of his athletic adventures ended. He could have given up entirely under the heading of *justifiable self-pity*... but he didn't.

With the help of Eleonor, he reentered politics at the age of 46, from the humbling position of a wheelchair and leg braces to eventually become president of the United States of America.[4] Little did he know that in eight years, he would be resurrecting that quote as we entered World War II (WWII) after the Japanese attacked Pearl Harbor.

So, what did it mean when he said that fear was the only thing we had to *fear*? During the Great Depression, people were afraid they wouldn't be able to feed their families or find a job. During the war, wives were afraid their husbands would be killed, and they wouldn't survive without them.

But they *did* feed their families, and most of the husbands *did* return, or the wives discovered they could obtain a job and raise their children alone. Do you get it?

---

3 Wikipedia Contributors, "Franklin D. Roosevelt," Wikipedia, The Free Encyclopedia, 2022, https://en.wikipedia.org/wiki/Franklin_D._Roosevelt.

4 Ibid.

What they were afraid of either never happened, or they found a way through it.

Fear really is the culprit that terrifies and paralyzes us. When we come face to face with a disturbing circumstance, fear tries to convince us that this is going to be the way it is forever. You may hear someone say, who is experiencing several bad events, "Welcome to my world," as if it will never change. The truth is, it's all in our minds, not in our reality.

Just ask the three prisoners that escaped from Alcatraz in 1962. That is, you might ask them if we knew where they were. When they entered Alcatraz, they were told by the guards, and the other inmates, that it was useless even to consider breaking out of the island prison, surrounded by icy waters and sharks. But they did it. We don't know if they made it all the way to land or not, but they didn't let the fear of what could happen keep them from trying.

Okay, so maybe escaped prisoners are not the best example to learn from, but it does make the point that fear causes us to give up before we even begin. In Matthew 8:23–26, we see Christ's disciples afraid; even though they were experienced sailors, they were fearful of the storm that arose on the sea that day.

My father loved to sail on Lake Erie. That may sound innocuous since it's a lake and not the ocean, but Lake Erie is notorious for its raging storms that would come out of nowhere. The rougher the waters, the more Dad enjoyed it. But he also knew when to beach his craft as the weather became threatening. I'm sure these disciples were of the same breed. They enjoyed a challenge, a rough sea now and then, but only when they knew they could handle it.

Verse 24 says that *the waves covered the ship*. If you've ever seen videos of Alaskan fishermen at sea hunting king crabs, you've seen men being swept off the deck by twenty-foot waves.

The worst fear I ever faced on the water was when I was about ten-years-old, on board a little fishing boat my father and brother had built. It had a small outboard motor bolted to the stern, which had an attached bar that also served as a rudder. We would take it out on Lake Erie, just off the shore, where my mother remained to prepare our picnic lunch.

I couldn't swim, but I did wear a life jacket. The blue sky was speckled with small puffy clouds. Bill and I dangled our hands in the water while my father stayed at the stern, keeping the rudder firmly on course. Without warning, our little craft began to rock sideways. A sudden wind had churned the lake into white caps, and my father's eyes began to enlarge. "Quick, Donna, get up at the bow and hang on!" Dad yelled, with the authority of a captain, "And, Bill, you get up there with your sister and hang on tight!"

The waves grew in size as the sky darkened. Suddenly, we were in the middle of one of those mysterious Lake Erie storms. Dad steered the boat directly into the waves, which, from my perspective, at the bow, made me sure we would capsize. Life jacket or not, I was certain I would drown.

The bow would rise above the horizon and then slam down on the water as if it hit a rock. I was fearful that the deck would shatter under my feet. I remember reciting the 23rd Psalm again and again. I was more than fearful; I was terrified. Then, just as quickly as it started... it stopped. We made it safely to shore, and I was grateful I knew a Bible verse that was able to give me hope in my time of fear.

In the Book of Matthew, the disciples had more than a verse to sustain them, they had Jesus on board, but the storm seemed overwhelming. Jesus said to them, as He calmed the sea, "O ye of little faith."[5] So, what did that mean? Was Jesus saying that if they had more faith, there wouldn't have been any storm? No. That can't be it because we see all kinds of storms in everyone's lives... from physical to environmental to spiritual... for nonbelievers as well as devout Christians.

I love one of the songs the Ball Brothers sing on their *Breakthrough* album, called, *Sometimes He Calms*

---

5 Matthew 8:26, KJV.

the Storm, *"and other times He calms His child."* **That's it!**
Sometimes *"He calms His child."*[6]

We want the storm to end. Occasionally that's what God does for us. He heals our illness or changes the path of the tornado. Over time, as we grow and mature in our walk with Jesus, He wants us to be able to lean on Him more and build more courage so that we can go through the trials that, inevitably, life dishes out—with a peace that passes all human understanding.

Fear begins in our minds. You may think it starts in the doctor's office, when he says you have cancer, or when you hear on the news that a major storm is on a destructive path through your town. But that's just words. The way you interpret those words is what goes on in your mind.

If David had translated the size and ferocity of Goliath as a treacherous enemy, who could not be defeated, the Philistines might have destroyed Israel. But they didn't because David ignored what he saw and heard, and he simply believed in God's Word.

Now, you can ignore bad news, but that won't change the fact that you have cancer or that the storm is headed your way. So, the best thing you can do is pray for God to change your thinking. Let Him help to strengthen you and show you some answers to your problem. Al-

6 "Sometimes He Calms the Storm Lyrics by The Ball Brothers," SongLyrics, 2022, https://www.songlyrics.com/the-ball-brothers/sometimes-he-calms-the-storm-lyrics/.

low Him to soothe your anxiety with His words from Scripture and with songs of praise, as Paul and Silas did while in prison.[7] Then, let God show His power over the problem.

Left to your own thoughts and plans, you will panic and freeze in your tracks. Depression could set in, and you could cripple your entire family by spreading your fears to them. Fear really is our biggest problem. Once we allow God's Word to change our thoughts, we can control our fears.

A member of our congregation was diagnosed with an aggressive cancer that was inoperable. She was in her sixties and had been a pastor at one time, now retired, but she didn't stop living. She went shopping with her friends, enjoyed short outings to fairs, and family gatherings. Whenever I saw her, she displayed a pleasant smile and would inquire as to how I was doing. At her funeral, I learned that whenever anyone asked her how she was dealing with her diagnosis, she would say, "If I live, it will be to the glory of God, and if I die, it will be to the glory of God." And it was.

Wow, she had definitely grown beyond the very human fear of death that most of us feel. Somehow, many Christians have come to believe that God wants us to have a cushiony life on earth, never getting sick or fac-

---

7 Acts 16:24-28.

ing problems and living forever and ever. Really? Where does it say that in God's Word?

As a parent, I don't want to raise a spoiled child. I don't want to keep him in some kind of safe bubble so that he never feels any hurt or sadness. He would grow up uncaring, without compassion, believing he is the most important person around. It is through the problems that we begin to understand others better. We grow in empathy. We can grow beyond fear because we have faced our fears, gone through our trials, and won.

Our church had members in small villages in Africa. When a large convention was planned for all the members to meet in one place, many had to walk for days to get there. They weren't expecting luxuries at these conventions, as many of us Americans might expect. They were only interested in meeting other brethren and hearing more of God's Word.

These gentle people rejoiced in having running water, cots to sleep on, and even cold showers. They were pleased to sit on the ground for some of the seminars. When the American pastors, who were serving them, said they would ask for prayers for this African congregation when they returned home, the pastors were surprised at their response. These non-materialistic but very happy Africans said they were praying for their American brethren. They felt that America had so many material blessings that it would be hard to appreciate the many ways that God was blessing them. Even though these people had to face persecution by their government, serious food shortages, and other personal hardships, they had grown beyond their fears and found the answer in the Word of God. While many American Christians seek material prosperity, a long and healthy life, and a life free from all problems as a reward for following Jesus, these Africans were passionately seeking Jesus.

Having defined what fear is, let's take a look at the many fears I had personally experienced, which may be similar to your own. Let's see if it's possible to get to the other side of fear and discover hope, joy, and peace in the midst of our trials.

CHAPTER 2

The Atomic Age

The thief comes only to steal and kill and destroy; I have come that they may have life, and have it to the full.

(John 10:10 NIV)

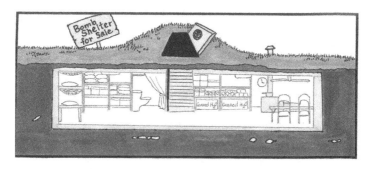

As you have heard on the news, nearly every country in our world has some form of nuclear warfare. Some want it to protect themselves from other nations, and others want to control other nations. It really doesn't matter because it's beyond our control. We can sit and worry about it, but there's nothing we can do to change it. So, how do we live under the shadow of this Atomic Age?

I was born near the end of World War II, in the small town of Bedford, near Cleveland, Ohio. The United States had entered the war in 1941, and by May of 1945, I was only two, my brother was seven, and my father was a robust twenty-nine-year-old. Dad didn't expect to be drafted because he was married with two children. While the United States had invaded Europe in June of 1944 with the hope of a swift surrender, it didn't happen. We were still fighting in Europe and the Pacific in the spring of 1945.

Unlike today, when America was at war in the 40s, all men, eighteen or over, were eligible to be drafted into the military. Even if you didn't have any able-bodied men in your household, everyone in the states had to deal with the rationing of gasoline, sugar, meat, and other materials. City folk were planting victory gardens in vacant lots in order to have some fresh vegetables for their table. Even the children were involved in the war effort by gathering scrap metals. Having already endured the Great Depression, my parents weren't feeling terribly deprived since they had been used to soup lines and job shortages. But the thought that my father might have to fight in the Pacific was terrifying.

While I was obviously, too young to understand the fear that my parents were facing, I learned later just how difficult it was for them. My father was drafted into the Army soon after President Roosevelt died in

April of 1945. Even though the war was dying down in Europe, my young father had to face his possible death in a ferocious battle on Japanese soil. I vaguely remember staying on my grandmother's farm in Ohio while mom went to be with my father in Florida's Camp Blanding for a final farewell and the signing of his last will and testament.

By the time his training was over and the men were being shipped out to the Pacific, President Harry Truman had ordered the dropping of two atomic bombs on Japan. Even though the war ended, a new fear was generated from the ashes of that conflict. We were now faced with the horrific after-effects of an atomic bomb.

We didn't have TVs in our homes until the late '50s, so most people saw the devastation of the cities of Hiroshima and Nagasaki and the fate of the Japanese people via the movie theater's news shorts or the newspaper. We learned that the ground couldn't produce anything for years, people were dying months and years later from nuclear fallout, and they discovered birth defects in children born after the war.

And yet, throughout the 1950s, we were being taught to "duck and cover". Our government actually thought that we could be spared in the event of a nuclear attack if we would just cover our faces and get under something solid, like our school desks. I remember marching to the basement of our school to kneel next to a wall and cover our faces from any blast of light. I don't remember any of us children taking it very seriously. It seemed to be just another fire drill. So, we just went through the motions.

By Junior High, we were issued dog tags. I guess the government felt the tags would survive a nuclear blast, even if we wouldn't. They could help identify the dead by collecting the tags. The truth is, the kids were using the tags as a "going steady" badge and exchanging them with their girlfriend or boyfriend.

America hadn't fully embraced the seriousness of this new bomb. We were still working off of our early WWII thinking that a bomb was limited in its scope. But atomic warfare was a whole new creation. We humans now have the potential to destroy the earth several times over. If that's not a reason to fear, I don't know what is.

People were building bomb shelters like folks now are building homes. They stocked them with preserved food and bedding and planned to lock their families in them until the nuclear fallout was over—months or even a year later, and then they would emerge with their families in tack. However, some very real questions arose. Who would you keep out of your underground ark? Your neighbor? Your brother? And what would be left to emerge into if everything and everyone was destroyed?

I started college in September of 1961. In October, I remember sitting on the edge of my roommate's bed when we heard a radio announcement that Russia had set off a gigantic thermonuclear bomb that was 3,333 times more devastating than the bomb that annihilated Hiroshima.[8] It had sent nuclear fallout into the upper atmosphere that would eventually encompass the entire earth, and we would all be feeling the effects of it within a month or so. We were freshmen who were just getting started on our quest to become teachers, and we were listening to news that could not only destroy our dream but our lives.

Strangely, we didn't panic. It was like all that foolish duck and cover training in our childhood had prepared us for such a threat. All we talked about was what we should do? At eighteen years of age, we discussed how we should use the few months left to us. Do we go home to be with our families for the last time or stay in college and carry on until such time as the end comes?

While that may sound morbid, it was in the back of the mind of many early *baby boomers*. It's what led to such frivolous and unruly behavior during the '60s. It is a kind of philosophy of *live today, for tomorrow you may die* or, as the hippies of that era phrased it, *make love, not war*. Peter, Paul and Mary, and other singers mournful-

---

8 Chris Pleasance, "Russia Releases Never-before-Seen Footage of the Tsar Bomba Test," Daily Mail Online, 2020, https://www.dailymail.co.uk/news/article-8665553/Russia-releases-never-seen-footage-Tsar-Bomba-test.html.

ly sang the youthful protests against the Viet Nam War with songs like *War, Who Needs It?* and *Where Have All the Flowers Gone?*

I stayed in college through all the turmoil and remained active in the off-campus church I attended at the time, going to services, singing in the choir, and participating in the singles activities they had for college attendees. That didn't make me perfect, and it didn't draw me into a closer relationship with God— that would come later, but it did keep me out of a lot of troubles, like drugs and the sexual freedom that was growing from the introduction of *the Pill*, approved by the FDA in June of 1960.[9]

By October of 1962, the world held its breath as the two superpowers had a showdown during what has become known as the Cuban Crisis.[10] Russia was bringing in ships loaded with nuclear warheads to be set up in Cuba, just ninety miles off the coast of Florida.[11] Russia denied it, and America was trying to prove it with surveillance planes and ships in the waters off Cuba. Interestingly, my brother was on a destroyer escort in those waters, and my future husband was flying in a seaplane

---

9 Elizabeth Siegel Watkins, "How Pill Became a Lifestyle Drug: The Pharmaceutical Industry and Birth Control in the United States since 1960," American Journal of Public Health 102 (8): 1462–72, https://doi.org/10.2105/AJPH.2012.300706.

10 Wikipedia Contributors, "Cuban Missile Crisis," Wikipedia, The Free Encyclopedia, 2022, https://en.wikipedia.org/wiki/Cuban_Missile_Crisis.

11 Ibid.

over the Russian ships that were slowly making their way to Cuba. Neither knew what they were looking for, nor that this was the very brink of what could have become World War III.

I was a sophomore, struggling with some of my classes, and my father was in the hospital when my mother called to say she was afraid for my brother's safety and my dad's health. She quickly reminded me that she was all alone. I listened, but there was nothing I could do. Somehow, I felt I was walking in the midst of the Serenity Prayer: "God grant me the serenity to accept the things I cannot change, the courage to change the things I can, and the wisdom to know the difference."[12] Wisdom was still a long way off, but courage was beginning to emerge... in place of fear. After a thirteen-day showdown, Russia removed its missiles from Cuba because President Kennedy held his ground and because Russia knew that we both had the bomb, and it could only lead to total annihilation for both sides.

This is the part that we often miss from our earthly vantage point because we can't see God at work; we tend to believe that God didn't know what was going on. The truth is, He was in control during the entire event. Man started the wars, built the nuclear weapons, and set up the confrontations... but God still had the final say. Re-

---

12 Wikipedia Contributors "Serenity Prayer," Wikipedia, The Free Encyclopedia, 2022, https://en.wikipedia.org/wiki/Serenity_Prayer.

member, even though God has given us the freedom to choose, He still can intervene when man goes too far—like in the time of Noah, the Tower of Babel, and Sodom and Gomorrah. It wasn't time to end this world in 1962, and worrying about it wasn't going to change anything.

That sobering threat was followed by the creation of several end-time movies, like *Fail-Safe, Dr. Strangelove,* and *On the Beach,* which raised a universal fear by their depiction of the obliteration of our planet if we continued to fight with such weapons. The subtitle of *Dr. Strangelove* was, *How I Learned to Stop Worrying and Love the Bomb.* While I can't say I learned to love the bomb, its threat was becoming a part of my daily routine. The closing song to that movie was, *We'll Meet Again, Don't Know Where, Don't Know When,* while a mushroom cloud was rising over the ocean.

That was my new world. It is our new world. One we don't want to think about because it says we are not in control—that we are going to die, sooner... or later.

For me, that brought my life into perspective. If I can't control everything or hardly anything, then I have to look to the One who can. I need to accept the fact that I will die sooner... or later. The good news is, as Paul wrote in Romans 8:18 (NIV), "I consider that our present sufferings are not worth comparing with the glory that will be revealed in us." So, we *will* meet again, no matter what happens on the earth. Surrounded by all the bad news today, *that* is a promise worth remembering.

In November 1963, as folks were beginning to accept life in this new Atomic Age, we witnessed the assassination of President Kennedy, played over and over again on the television in our dorm lobby. Some young adults wanted to quit school, feeling like the world was coming to an end. Others wanted to run away from this world that the adults had made, so they got into drugs and even communes. Some joined the military or the Peace Corps to change the world, but I joined the group who felt there was something that we could do to improve our little corner of the world, right here at home.

Churches stayed open 24/7 to accommodate all the new attendees looking for direction in those troubled times. As is unfortunately true, during many other difficult times, the church attendance dropped when the people felt the problems had ceased, or at least had lessoned and were more manageable.

When Tom Brokaw wrote *The Greatest Generation* in 1998, I felt it was not fair to all the millions of people before and after that generation. I grant you that many from the Great Depression and WWII deserve recognition.

But the *greatest* generation means that everyone in that generation was doing the right thing, wasn't afraid to serve or support their neighbor when things got tough, and that's just not true. No entire generation can say they did everything right. So, I would rather Mr. Brokaw had titled his book, *Some Extraordinary People.*

We all have the potential to be extraordinary. It's how we deal with the situations we find ourselves in, not the generation we were born into, that matters. Each generation has its unique challenges. The only way we can do anything great is to stay in God's Word and keep communicating with Him daily and, thus, get to the other side of our fears.

So, how does war, nuclear annihilation, and our lack of control over everything around us help us grow beyond fear? It takes your attention off what you can do because you begin to see that you can't really do anything except pray. And that makes you humble, the very place you need to be if God is going to work with you and through you. It also takes death and dying out of the fear equation because it is so obviously inevitable. We have to surrender to God's will and then, through His teachings, find the strength and courage we never knew we had.

CHAPTER 3

Higher Education

A wise person is hungry for knowledge, while
the fool feeds on trash.

(Proverbs 15:14 NLT)

I don't know about you, but when I finished high
school, I really didn't want to go to college or even an oc-
cupational training school. I was a fairly good student.
I even made the honor society. Being a girl who had just
turned eighteen, I didn't think I could get into a career.

My ambition was to work as a waitress. I had worked
part-time in restaurants since I was sixteen. That was
my comfort zone. I figured I would date for a while until

I met Mr. Right. It was 1961, most young women hadn't thought about careers unless you classified being married and staying home to raise your children as a career.

I never considered reading to be one of my strong points, and I was tired of cramming for exams. But my father had other ideas. He saw my potential and insisted that I pick out a college and a future vocation. You can imagine how that made me feel. I hated the idea. Mostly because I didn't think I could make it, surrounded by a bunch of eggheads, as we referred to the smart kids back then.

A lot of my teachers said that colleges were more challenging than they had been. An "A" student in high school would be a "C" student in college. I had managed a "B" average, so I was already doomed.

No one in our family had gone to college. My brother chose the Navy and then took a correspondence course to attain his engineering degree. Mom had an eighth-grade education, and my father had earned his high school diploma, but now he wanted me to go, where no one else had gone—kind of like being on *Star Treks'* Enterprise. I was scared.

In my first year, I received one "A," several "Cs," and a "D" in art appreciation. Art was always my strongest subject. I was shocked. But even more shocking than that was an "F" in American History. I loved history. I had studied very hard, but there it was. I knew it. I wasn't college material. I was ready to throw in the towel.

Once again, my dad had other ideas. "You're not going to be a quitter. What do you have to do to make up for that 'F'?" I whined a little and then said, "I won't be able to get my diploma until I take the course again and get at least a "C". I can't add that horrible class to my normal schedule. I'd need to take it in the summer, and I need a break. I don't want to go to summer school."

So, that summer, I was back on the campus, in an un-air-conditioned classroom and dormitory room, literally sweating it out. Steve Allen, the comedian, had a late-night TV show back then in which he would just crack up a bit and shout, "Shmock! Shmock!" It seemed like a fitting relief for all of us summer school prisoners to shout from our dorm windows. So, in the middle of the night, from all the corners of my campus, one could hear the strange sounds of some foreign birds echoing, "Shmock! Shmock! Shmock!" It helped put a smile on our faces before someone shouted, "Shut up, I'm trying to sleep."

I hated taking classes in the summer, but I did manage to get a "C," and I was just a little proud of myself for not quitting. Of course, I wasn't about to tell my father that.

I kept plodding along, enjoying some classes, enduring others. I had completed one semester of student teaching with a delightful kindergarten teacher, who gave me an "A" in my junior year, but in my senior year, I had a really strict teacher in a fifth-grade classroom who nitpicked over the pronunciation of nearly every word I said. When it came down to her final grade for this last student teaching experience, she asked me to come to her office.

"Donna, I've watched you closely. You know you made a lot of mistakes in handling the making of a Pilgrim village, but you didn't quit; you got through it. You still seem to have trouble pronouncing some words properly. And I'm torn between giving you an 'A' or an 'F'."

My continence dropped. I held back the tears and tried to look unaffected by her words. She was not the kind of woman you could argue with, so I remained silent.

"I'll have to think about this some more." With that, she dismissed me. If she gave me an "F," it would, no doubt, set back my graduation and thus any chance of getting hired as a teacher.

In addition to that challenge, our college had become a university, and we were required to have a minor to graduate. My major was elementary education, and the only minor I had enough credits for at that point was social studies, my worst subject. Consequently, I was forced to choose a course in the field I was most afraid of in order to obtain my diploma.

The only class that I had any interest in was anthropology (the study of human societies and cultures). I really didn't know what it was all about, but I had been interested in becoming a paleontologist when I was young (that's someone who unearths old bones). Anyhow, I went into that class with gusto. I took meticulous notes and then went home to copy them neatly on my typewriter, even typing some important points in red ink (which, in those days, was on the typewriter ribbon; you just had to push down a key to change the color). I even sketched pictures of any Cro-Magnon men that the instructor drew on the blackboard.

My notes turned out so good the professor held my notebook up to show the class. Little did he know how desperate I was to pass his course, and I only created the notebook to prepare for his tests. By facing the fear of that class, instead of giving up, I was able to close my college record with an "A" in anthropology, and my student teaching instructor finally decided to do the same.

Interestingly, after all these years, I've come to enjoy reading. And I've finally started writing several books. The real topper is I actually have toyed with the thought of going back to college, probably online, to achieve a master's degree. At seventy-nine, I don't know how much good it would do me, except make my name look a little more important on any future books I wrote. People seem to be more impressed with what you have to say if you have an MBA, MD, or Ph.D. after your name.

The fact is that everyone has some knowledge that might benefit someone else. Titles aren't what defines us or our importance. We all have something to say if we'd just lean on God for the courage to say it.

Will Rogers was an actor, cowboy, humorist, and newspaper columnist. He had a tenth-grade education but never stopped learning. Every morning, it is said, he would read several newspapers to gather material for his political humor. He also met with several dignitaries and presidents. His quotes are still used today because they are ageless, and he did it all while calmly twirling a lasso and speaking with a western drawl.

Mother Teresa reached her universal fame by being compassionate and caring for the poor, forgotten, and unloved in society.[13] John D. Rockefeller dropped out of high school to become a bookkeeper. He later founded Standard Oil and became one of the richest men in history.[14] Thomas Edison attended a few months of formal schooling and then was homeschooled by his mother. He was always curious and an avid reader. He has been credited for the invention of the incandescent light bulb, the phonograph, the storage battery, and the

---

13 Judy Ponio, "How Mother Teresa Changed the World - Our Father's House Soup Kitchen," Our Father's House Soup Kitchen, 2021, https://ofh-soupkitchen.org/mother-teresa-charity.

14 The Editors of Encyclopaedia Britannica, "John D. Rockefeller," In Encyclopaedia Britannica, 2021, https://www.britannica.com/biography/John-D-Rockefeller.

movie camera, as well as over a thousand patents.[15] Bill Gates dropped out of college and revolutionized the Tech Industry.[16]

Higher education is not an absolute necessity for everyone. Without a goal for what you want to do in your future, higher education can be a waste of your time and money. But if you want to be a teacher, lawyer, doctor, etc., there is no way around it. You have to obtain a college diploma.

If you really love building ships, then you might become an apprentice to an accomplished shipbuilder. We need shoemakers, glass blowers, electricians, chefs, plumbers, truck drivers, and barbers. While it may require a few months of training or working under someone else, it may not require college.

All I'm saying is, don't go to college because someone said you had to, but don't avoid college because of any fear you may have about succeeding. Go because it's essential to your lifetime goal. Get purpose-focused... not *fear*-focused... and you will succeed.

---

15 "Thomas Alva Edison," In Development of the Industrial U.S. Reference Library, Encyclopedia.Com, 2018, https://www.encyclopedia.com/people/science-and-technology/electrical-engineering-biographies/thomas-alva-edison.

16 Benjamin Waterhouse, "Tech Giants: Steve Jobs and Bill Gates," Bill of Rights Institute, 2022, https://billofrightsinstitute.org/essays/tech-giants-steve-jobs-and-bill-gates.

CHAPTER 4

Marriage

The LORD God said, "It is not good for the
man to be alone. I will make a helper suitable
for him."

(Genesis 2:18 NIV)

Getting married can be a scary proposition, especially when you see beautifully orchestrated weddings
that look like a dream come true, at least for the bride.
Then you watch it fall apart in as little as a year and end
in an angry divorce that leaves both individuals bitter.
Is it any wonder that many couples think they have the
answer to the problem by choosing to live together be-

fore marriage to see if it's going to work for them? Some never want to get married because they've seen thirty-year marriages also coming to an end. We had one such couple who had joined our church. They had lived together for twenty years, raised their son, and finally decided to get married, with their son as their best man.

Just look at Princess Diana and Prince Charles. It was a fairy tale romance, a picture-perfect wedding, and a future of financial security and endless happiness. How can anything so lovely wind up so ugly?

None of us want to find out that love has died. We never wanted to be in a custody battle over the children, the very offspring we hoped would draw us closer together.

Without the Bible as our compass, we take off on an unknown journey to meet the right partner, but often for the wrong reasons. We want them to be attractive, funny, and provide all our needs. Their character and morals are often the last things on our list.

It reminds me of one of the shows that aired on *Happy Days*, where the Fonz takes out a list of the perfect woman for him. I don't recall all of her attributes, but the list focused almost entirely on her physical appearance. Humorous as that was, isn't that what most of us want in our future mates, especially when we are young?

At twenty-two, after graduating from college, I had hoped to at least be engaged. Unfortunately, I wasn't even pinned, as was the custom of the fraternities on campus. In the sixties, there still were die-hards who wanted marriage but didn't really have a clue as to how to find Mister or Miss Right. So, my first desire was to secure my independence by finding my own apartment and even moving to another state. Funny how God had other plans for me.

Since a beginning teacher's salary, back in 1965, was less than $5000 a year, and I had a car to pay for along with my room and board; I did what many young people did, I moved in with my parents. I was able to find a teaching position close to where they lived, which was in Moon Township, near the Greater Pittsburgh Airport.

I had dated in college, but marriage didn't seem to be on the mind of most of the men I met. Sex before marriage, or not marrying at all, was becoming the trend. *One-night stands* became a familiar phrase. Promiscuity was on the rise, and while I enjoyed some of the dates with dancing and a movie, I had hoped to meet a more serious gentleman who might want more than just a good time.

Coming back to my parent's home didn't help any. By now, most of the guys I knew were either in the military or married, and the ones I was meeting either were divorced or had the same ideas as the guys on my campus.

I tried the new singles scene of going to what was called 21 Clubs. Live rock bands entertained the young patrons. Meanwhile, you had to strain to listen to the waitress ask, "What would you like to drink?" over the pounding drums and electric guitars. This was not exactly conducive to having any meaningful conversations.

I went with a couple of my girlfriends, but we all agreed that the caliber of the guys we met there were not what we were looking for or interesting. I remember thinking to myself, *If you're going to meet in a bar, don't be surprised if you wind up married to a drunk.* Alcoholism ran on my father's side of the family. While my dad didn't have the problem, others did, and it destroyed their marriage, jobs, and health.

So, I came up with a new idea. If the right guys weren't out there... then maybe I needed to find a way to bring them in here, into the church. The church I was attending had a teen coffee shop but no singles group. When I tried to convince our minister to start one, he said, "The young people today won't come. They are meeting in bars and tend to avoid church." I knew that, but that was the very reason I felt the church needed at least to try out the idea. He reluctantly granted me a room to meet in on Sunday afternoons.

I already knew most of the singles because I had met them when I attended there with my parents over the past decade. It was fun catching up with some of them, but we were more like brothers and sisters than future husbands or wives. We put together fun activities, like going out to dinner at specialty restaurants or ice skating at a local rink, but no one wanted to get involved in any outreach ideas I had.

As winter approached, new members began to join us from outside our normal circle of friends. We gathered together for some winter sports and parties. By the end of the year, wedding bells claimed four of our members. When September rolled around, I wasn't sure I wanted to pursue it anymore... and that's when I received a phone call.

It seems a young pilot had just moved into the area and was hoping to join a singles group in the Presbyterian church. Our pastor told him to call me to see if we were going to continue with the group. He and I talked for about two hours. He seemed interested in the fact that I was a teacher, and I found it interesting how he became a pilot. We even speculated that education would be so much more interesting if, instead of always learning from a book or lecture, a student could travel to the place about which he had been reading. Needless to say, I agreed to open up the group for another year, and he agreed to come to our next meeting. We clicked so well on the phone that I was almost afraid to meet him, for fear he wouldn't look as good as he sounded. When we did meet, I was pleasantly surprised.

He came in wearing a sports jacket and tie. He cut a trim six-foot figure, and with his dark military haircut, I felt he was a thirty-year-old father looking for his children's classroom. Instead, he looked at me and said, "I'm Nelson Trickett, and I'm looking for the singles meeting."

"Oh, Nelson, I'm Donna Killip, the one you were talking to on the phone. Welcome, we're just about to begin."

All the girls in our group liked what they saw, and I was sure that he would pick one of them, and I'd be back to the question of whether or not to continue with our group. Sure enough, all these girls began their female maneuvers with things like, "Nelson, could you give me a lift back to my place?"

While we talked a little, he never asked me out. In fact, he hadn't asked any of the girls out on a date that autumn. He did attend the outings and enjoyed their company, but he didn't ask anyone on a date.

Then, on a very cold Sunday, on the first of January, as we were exiting the church parking lot, waiting our turn to get out, his car pulled up next to mine. I rolled down my window, and we had a short chat.

"Are you coming to the pastor's get-together at his house this evening?" I asked.

"No, I didn't know about it. When is it?"

"Six o'clock."

"I had planned to visit my folks in Utica during my days off," he replied.

"You could still visit them and enjoy the social this afternoon. In fact," I added with my own female wiles, "it will give you a chance to see the Monongahela Wharf and all the Christmas lights reflecting in the river at the Point."

Now, if you are familiar with Pittsburgh, the Wharf is just a lower paved parking lot that often is flooded in the winter by the converging rivers of the Monongahela, Allegheny, and the Ohio. Mt. Washington was more of a sightseeing place or even the Duquesne incline, but I had to think fast, and the Wharf was the best I could come up with.

Just then, the traffic began to move, and he said, "I'll think about it," as he drove away.

I no longer lived near the airport because my folks had moved to an apartment, across the river, in Sewickley. The church and the minister's home were near each other and not far from Nelson's apartment, which was within walking distance of the airport and the church.

At about four o'clock, Nelson called me to ask for directions to the minister's home. He had decided to attend the party. And what did I reply? "It would be easier if you came over here to get me, and I'll direct you to the minister's home."

He drove the five miles to my residence, and what was to be a few hours at the pastor's home, turned into a date that lasted into the wee hours of the morning—even taking in the Monongahela Wharf and window shopping along the streets of the city.

I learned a lot about Nelson on that first accidental date. He hadn't dated a lot. His prime attention after high school was on acquiring his pilot license and landing a job with an airline. He was twenty-seven and had done his stint in the Navy. And something else that really piqued my interest was that he enjoyed the minister's two little girls. He did some simple hand tricks for them, and it made them giggle. I hadn't seen the tender side of any other guy I dated. Being an elementary teacher, I liked what I saw.

After three months of meeting both of our families, dating nearly every night, attending various functions, from weddings to square dances—we were engaged, and by August of that year, we were married.

But I don't want to lead you to believe that it was all *happily ever after*. No marriage has a fairy tale ending. That's one of the misconceptions we perpetrate in the movies and dating shows. You meet, fall in love, and as the Beatles sang, *All You Need Is Love*. When you marry young, and that includes being in your twenties, or for the wrong reasons, like self-gratification or money, you really don't fully understand the meaning of love.

One quote I wrote down in a journal I kept before I was married stated that there was a middle-aged woman who had been married for thirty years and had five children. When asked what love was, she said, "It's what you've been through together." How true, how true.

It's the tears, the forgiveness, the good times, the bad times that really grow the love between two people. It's not having lots of fun all the time. Many people think that the more fun things they have in common with their partner, the stronger the bond. Just ask the band of brothers that is formed by many ground troops in war zones. They were bound by trust and having each other's back in the hard times, when their very lives were threatened, not by going from one party to the next.

The Bible says...

It is better to go to the house of mourning than to go to the house of feasting...

(Ecclesiastes 7:2 NIV)

You probably want to avoid funerals, right? But if you only go where people are partying all the time, you may find yourself in the company of alcohol abusers, drug users, or just unreliable friends that don't want to support you when you need them the most.

Nelson loved to fly; I loved to draw. He enjoyed skiing, but I enjoyed ice skating. He loved keeping things neat, and I often created messes. How did we ever get together, let alone stay together for fifty-three years?

Compromise, forgiveness, trying new things, allowing him to do his thing while I did mine. But something even more important to our marital bond is that we both desired a closer relationship with God, we loved to help people, and we both loved children.

In the beginning of a marriage, the wedding day is the icing on the cake. The selection of the bride's gown, cake, bridesmaids, and meal, often takes more time to select than the bride took to find the right husband. It's actually a bit like putting the cart before the horse. More money is spent on the wedding day and honeymoon than on a down payment for their future home. There needs to be more time spent building a foundation for a good marriage than planning the wedding day celebration.

Both of our parents had eloped during the Great Depression, when big weddings were unheard of, at least for the middle and lower classes. My mother only had a new dress and a corsage to celebrate the event. Nelson's parents remained married until his father's death, over fifty-two years later, and my parents were married for sixty years until my dad died. Both were married by a Justice of the Peace in humble beginnings, but both couples were dedicated to their vows.

When I got engaged, Mom took over the planning of my wedding as if it were her own. I was okay with that because I knew how much it meant to her, and I really just wanted to marry Nelson. I did choose the colors for our wedding day and my bouquet. Plus, it was really special and unique because many of my past fourth-grade students attended and flanked both sides of the altar during the ceremony.

A lasting marriage begins when the two learn more about each other and bond more closely to God than to things, and that takes time. Don't be afraid to invest time and energy, and even a little money, into your marriage.

God granted my husband and me fifty-three years together to get it right. Each year grew a little better than the last—even though trials seemed inevitably to latch on at different stages, we didn't run away; we faced them together.

CHAPTER 5

Childbirth

Children are a heritage from the LORD, off-spring a reward from him.

(Psalm 127:3 NIV)

While most men see the birth of their child as a product of their virility and a reason to settle down, make more money, and plan for their child's future, women often have a different view. Every woman wants to have a baby, at least most women feel that way, but there is a fear connected with childbirth that many young women don't want to discuss.

The PBS network has carried a series entitled, *Call the Midwife*. It reenacts scenes in England, starting at the end of WWII and beyond, when many women didn't have access to a hospital, and they had their babies at home, with a midwife present. Each birth is different, of course, but each mother-to-be had concerns for either the baby, herself, or both. Most fathers were often asked to leave the room during the labor and delivery.

We rarely see any midwives today, and many things have changed for the expectant mother since the 1940s. We now have birthing rooms in hospitals that allow the father to be present and even allow the baby to remain in the room with the mother after the delivery. But first-time moms, in particular, still enter into labor with some apprehension. They desire to have a baby, but they are bombarded with advice and fears that grow more and more ominous as the big day arrives. And if the mother has any health problems herself, like diabetes, her concerns are even more disturbing.

As natural as childbirth is, occasionally, something does go wrong. So, it is important that an expectant mother takes precautions with what she eats and the activities she engages in so that her child can have the best chance to live a normal, healthy life.

When a young woman finally delivers her child, there is a certain pride that exudes from her continence because she realizes she has overcome her fears and any discomfort during the contractions in order to hold that miraculous bundle in her arms.

Sadly, with all the exuberance most men feel at the birth of their offspring, they will never know that feeling the Bible describes in John 16:21.

> A woman giving birth to a child has pain because her time has come; but when her baby is born, she forgets the anguish because of her joy that a child is born into the world.
>
> (NIV)

For some young women, this is the first real fear they have had to face, and even with caring individuals wrapped around her, she has to go through it alone. It's her pushes and determination that births her child.

If you are anticipating your first child and you have concerns of any kind, get informed, do whatever you can to help you and your baby, and... most importantly, rest in the promises of God's Word because He will be there from the inception to the delivery. Build your relationship with Him, and you will come to enjoy your pregnancy and the delivery more than you ever thought possible. You'll find yourself stronger than you thought you were, and you will be happier than you could ever imagine.

I hadn't relied on God as much as I relied on my doctor when I was expecting our first child. You see, my mother had told me the story of my brother's birth ever since I could remember. Mom had my brother in the house of her in-laws. Because my grandmother was a nurse, she felt she could manage to be a midwife to my mother without any help from the doctor. Since she worked, back in the day, with rather primitive methods of handling mentally ill patients, who resisted treatment, she tied my mother's hands and feet to the bedpost. I know. That was a revolting image for me to contemplate, too.

When the delivery wasn't going as planned, they called the doctor, who, in those days, actually came to the house. He helped deliver my brother with forceps. He had anticipated that my mother was going to have some problems because of a truck accident she was in when she was younger. But my grandmother hadn't known about it and took matters into her own hands.

Like John 16:21 stated, my mother never looked back on Bill's birthday as a tragedy. Instead, she immediately planned to give birth again—as it turned out, it was to have me. Years later, her pride in the strength she showed on my brother's birthday made her want to review the difficulty of that birth, again and again. It's like a soldier who, years after his war experience on the front lines, wants to tell the story over and over because it's one of the bravest times in his life.

For that reason, it's good not to listen to all the birthing stories unless they are encouraging. We all are a bit of a storyteller. So, don't be surprised when a mom hears or sees that you are expecting, that they may offer you unwanted advice that is more disturbing than helpful. I mean, if a mother is telling you how difficult it is to give birth, why did she have two or more children? Why didn't she stop with one?

Anyhow, my mother unwittingly planted fear in me about having children. And after experiencing painful menstrual cycles, I was sure that childbirth would be unbearable. Then, when I met Nelson and saw how he enjoyed children, I knew that I would have to reconsider my long-held conviction against pregnancy.

I never wanted to consider an abortion, so I had contemplated being an old maid school teacher. It had been a common practice that female teachers were not allowed to be married during the turn of the last century. I thought I could handle that since I would always be surrounded by children... but then I fell in love. Marriage without children would not be such a good idea. Even if we couldn't have one of our own, I would definitely consider adoption. So, I knew I had to plan for children in our upcoming marriage.

I went for a doctor's exam before getting married to be sure I didn't have any physical problem, like my mother, that would prevent a natural birth. I was fine. Then, after five months into our marriage, I found myself sad that I wasn't pregnant. Me, the one who had been afraid to become pregnant or even get married, was extremely disappointed that I couldn't get pregnant. God can do strange things with your mind... if you let Him.

In February, of all people, a dentist asked if I was pregnant. Somehow, he arrived at that finding due to the condition of my gums. He said that I should see a medical doctor. The M.D. confirmed that I was expecting but cautioned me not to overstrain myself because I had some spotting.

I finished my school year and sweated through the hot summer in anticipation of the birth of our first child. In the late sixties, we didn't have sonograms to check the baby's gender, so I didn't know for sure if it would be a boy or girl. I also didn't know about Lamaze or La Leche League classes for expectant mothers. My prayers were just that God would make my baby healthy... that's all.

Kirk came a little early, at 4 lbs. 13 oz. I was expecting the hospital to knock me out, so I wouldn't feel anything, but since this was a premature birth, the doctor didn't want to give me any anesthetics. So, without any preparation beforehand, I was awake through an entire natural delivery until the doctor saw his head. Then they knocked me out and cleaned him up.

When I woke up, I only saw our son's crying head peeking out of the warm receiving blanket. I hadn't touched him or counted his fingers and toes. They just whisked him out of the room in one direction and took me to my room in the opposite direction.

For hospital precautionary reasons, he was immediately put into an incubator. The next morning, with Nelson by my side, we went to see our new son inside the walls of his incubator. He was crying and pushing himself towards the glass walls, proving that he didn't need the extra help, but he did need to be loved.

Within an hour, he was taken out of the glass cubical and brought to me to feed him with a bottle. The hospital had already determined that I would not be breastfeeding my baby. I was told I had fifteen minutes to feed the tiny bottle of formula into him before they took him back to the nursery. If he stopped sucking, I was to rap the bottom of his foot with my fingernail. Every cry tore at my heart. I wanted to hold him, not scold him.

This is not to make any of you afraid to go to the hospital to deliver your child. As I said earlier, hospitals have made birthing a family-friendly, cozy time where you can relax while the nurses see to all your needs. But the late '60s still had a long way to go in that area.

So, when I was pregnant with our second child, I opted to have her at home. By the early '70s, things were beginning to change. After my first experience, I wanted to have more control over my child and more time to bond as a mother and a family.

I found a doctor that was willing to do a home delivery. While many family members and friends thought

I was crazy, I did have some supporters, including my husband, who were willing to help me prepare for the event.

I attended Lamaze classes and learned to control my breathing. In La Leche League meetings, I learned how to have a successful breastfeeding experience. At home, I was taking daily walks with our now three-year-old son, and I went over a checklist of all the equipment we would need to make the birthing experience safe and enjoyable. Nelson was able to help in the delivery, the doctor was present, and Kimberly was born healthy, weighing in at eight-and-a-half pounds.

Again, I am not advocating that you plan to have your child at home, especially when the hospitals today are offering you such comfortable surroundings and support by even allowing the husband to participate in the birthing process. I'm merely trying to tell you that childbirth is a natural thing. Children have been born in the field, on airplanes, in the back of a taxi, at home, or, as most families choose today, in a birthing room at the hospital.

Life has no guarantees, but you can't worry about every shadow that presents itself in challenging situations. You need to remember that God wants you to grow stronger and put fear aside, as He watches over you in your hour of need.

CHAPTER 6

Airline Travel

> But when I am afraid, I will put my confidence in you. Yes, I will trust the promises of God. And since I am trusting him, what can mere man do to me?
>
> (Psalm 56:3–4 TLB)

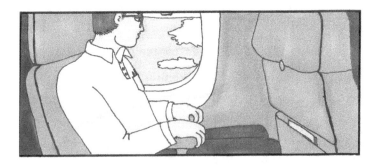

For thousands of years, man has traveled rather slowly on horseback, in carriages, or sailing on board a ship. It wasn't until the first steam locomotive hauled passengers in 1825 that men began to cross greater distances more quickly.[17] Many were afraid to ride on this

---

17 "George Stephenson's First Steam Locomotive," History Today, 2022, https://www.historytoday.com/archive/george-stephensons-first-steam-locomotive.

strange iron horse because it went so fast, and it looked rather threatening.

By 1885, the first horseless carriage, otherwise known as the automobile, was invented.[18] Less than twenty years after that, the first, rather flimsy, aircraft made its maiden voyage in 1903 at Kitty Hawk, North Carolina.[19] It took quite a while for that glorified kite, which could only take one passenger and travel at about 6.8 mph, to grow into the size of today's Airbus, which can transport over 800 passengers and travel over 600 mph.[20] [21]

So, it's no wonder that there are skeptics out there who do not want to fly. They aren't sure that it has been thoroughly tested.

Will Smith, the actor/comedian, has a YouTube video of jumping out of an airplane for the very first time. He speaks about his fear leading up to it, but then he says the following: "The point of maximum danger, is the point of minimum fear (and) God placed the best things in life, on the other side of fear."[22]

---

18 "Karl Benz," The American Society of Mechanical Engineers, 2022, https://www.asme.org/topics-resources/content/karl-benz.

19 "115 Years Ago: Wright Brothers Make History at Kitty Hawk," National Aeronautics and Space Administration, 2021, https://www.nasa.gov/feature/115-years-ago-wright-brothers-make-history-at-kitty-hawk.

20 Ibid.

21 Eric Rosenberg, "Fastest Airplanes Commercial Passengers Can Fly." NerdWallet, 2021, https://www.nerdwallet.com/article/travel/fastest-airplanes-commercial-passengers-can-fly.

22 "Will Smith and His First Skydiving Experience," SkyXtreme.Tv, 2022, https://skyxtreme.tv/what-skydiving-taught-me-about-fear-storytime/.

Can that be? Are the best things in life a part of overcoming our fears? It certainly seems that way, in the previous examples of marriage and childbirth. But what about flying? Man wasn't meant to fly, right?

The Bible doesn't say anything about a man driving 65 mph in a car, either, but we do. Change is life. When you cease to accept change, you die. Not necessarily in the physical, but in your vitality and perspective of life. True, lots of changes today are morally unacceptable and moving at breakneck speeds. Modern inventions are always being upgraded and can be irritating and time-consuming, but that doesn't mean they are evil.

It's like fire. Fire can keep you warm. Most people love to have a crackling fire gently burning in their fire-place on a cold wintery night. But a fire that gets out of hand, like the wildfires on the west coast, is totally un-acceptable and fearful. So, the issue is not whether fly-ing is a good thing or not; it is how it is used or misused.

Just ask William Shatner, age ninety, of *Star Trek*, who became the oldest person to go into space in Oc-tober of 2021. After he returned to earth, he said, "This experience is something unbelievable. I hope I never re-cover from this."[23]

William Shatner played Captain Kirk on the Star-ship, Enterprise for years on TV. But now, taking the

---

23 Harwood, William, "William Shatner Sets Record in Space with Blue Origin Spaceflight," CBS News Interactive Inc., 2021, https://www.cbsnews.com/live-updates/william-shatner-blue-origin-space-flight/.

risk of going into actual space with no guarantees of his safe return, he speaks of an experience so exceptional that he never wants to forget it.

That's how I felt when Nelson, my then boyfriend, took me up in a borrowed Cessna, through an opening in the clouds, to witness a bird's eye view of our earth for the first time in my life. And that's how I felt when our family left chilly northwestern Pennsylvania to arrive on the island of Hawaii, surrounded by tropical flowers, warm off-shore breezes, and the unique sound of steel guitars playing soft romantic tunes. Was it worth any risk that might be associated with flying? Absolutely.

We often speak of the things we want to do before we die as our bucket list. There was even a movie by that name, which depicted two men with inoperable cancer, choosing to do everything they ever dreamed of in the few days they had left to live. Not to spoil the ending if you haven't seen the movie, but each man discovers that the best thing in life, really is his family. I agree.

If you ever have a chance to travel by air, it will almost certainly add joy to your family's memories. Does that mean you should become a risk-taker? Yes and no.

I see the adrenalin rush that two storm-chasers got from running after tornados, so they could gather statistics about how these storms began. That's a part of their job, and their risk-taking attitude helps them do what they need to do. The same is true with many firefighters who go into burning buildings to rescue someone, or our military, who serve on the ground in dangerous places. If they didn't do what they do, taking risks, we would suffer greatly.

On the other side of risk-taking are those who do it with harmful intentions, like the street racing that took place in the '50s. Teenagers would speed down a road, trying to win a race that could end in someone's death. They didn't even have seatbelts to protect them. Seeking danger just to get an adrenalin rush is not such a good idea. But not flying to a family event or for your job requirements because you're afraid to fly, is not such a good idea, either. It is crippling you from going forward, from fully enjoying the life God has given you.

Needless to say, being married to a commercial pilot, I had to overcome any hesitation I may have had about flying. I even had to go as far as to embrace it if we were to go forward on common ground.

Many people thought I was very brave to see my husband off on a trip that might take him through a storm or a mechanical failure, and he would never come home. I saw the plane crashes on the news. I wasn't blind to the possible dangers... but in all the twenty-eight years that Nelson flew and I flew with him, we never encountered a life-threatening experience.

On the other hand, I was in seven car accidents, two of which totaled the car and one took the life of our daughter, but I continued to drive a car. We'll get into the details of those experiences in the following chapter.

My point is... traffic accidents are so frequent that we only hear of the most serious crashes because it would take the entire day to report all the car wrecks in any one state. Airplane accidents are much less frequent, but because they involve many passengers from other states or countries, they receive more media attention.

If car accidents are more frequent than airplane accidents, why do you still drive or go places as a passenger in a car? Right. I get it. Cars help you to get where you need to go. The same is true with the airplane, which is still the safest means of travel.

Once again, it may help to review Will Smith's quote, that *"the best things lie on the other side of fear."* I wrote an entire book of the best things that we, as a family, experienced because of our airline travels. It's titled, *How to RELAX While Flying.* Allow me to take several stories from that book to make my point about airline travel and fear.

One chapter mentions flying in a hot air balloon over Monticello, the home of our late president, Thomas Jefferson, in Charlottesville, Virginia. I know a balloon isn't an airplane, but it helps make my point.

We were actually having a rare road-trip vacation from Ohio to Virginia Beach. It was getting late, and we were tired when we pulled off the Blue Ridge Parkway to find a hotel. As we drove up to the gate of the historic, Boar's Head Inn, an employee asked if we were interested in taking a hot air balloon ride the next morning. My flying ace, husband, immediately responded, "Yes," and then turned to his half-asleep wife and asked, "What do you say, dear? Do you want to take a balloon ride?"

I mumbled, "Yeah, sure."

At about four a.m., I bolted upright in bed and wondered if I had dreamed the event or not. So, I woke Nelson to ask, "Did you sign us up for a balloon ride this morning?"

As he pried his eyes open, he replied, "Ah, yeah. Won't that be great? But we don't have to be in the parking lot until six a.m., so go back to sleep."

"Sleep, are you kidding? I'm not going up in any balloon. We don't know anything about the guy who's flying it. A balloon can't be controlled like an airplane. No, I can't do this."

"Honey, you're getting yourself all worked up for nothing. This is a professional balloon pilot, and he won't go up if anything is out of order, no more than I would with my aircraft."

I could see there was no changing his mind. I just laid awake, anticipating the worst.

When we got to the parking lot, there were other people waiting for the adventure to begin. We had to help inflate the balloon and, because there were so many of us, we had to take turns. It was decided that Nelson, Kirk, and I were to ride in the chase van, tracking the balloon, as it floated across the countryside. It only caused me to feel more anxious, as I anticipated the balloon crashing into some trees or someone tumbling out of the basket when it hit some air turbulence. Funny how our minds can conjure up the worst scenarios when fear begins to take hold of us.

Kirk was already working towards his private pilot license, so he and his dad were beaming with excitement as the first travelers landed safely in the open field. Now, it was our turn.

After helping me over the side of the wicker basket, we were given helmets to protect us from the flame out whenever the pilot needed to raise the balloon. I grabbed hold of the basket and held on for dear life as we began to ascend. The noise of the flame was a little disturbing, but there was no jerking or weaving. We just floated up and up until we were well above the chase car and the surrounding homes.

Once the balloon reached the height the pilot wanted, he turned off the flame. It was totally quiet. We were a part of the gentle breeze as we watched birds winging along with us. When some people on the ground saw us, they waved, and we could hear everything they said, even when they didn't shout. I could see why these balloons were used during the Civil War to spy on enemy troops at night. Soon, we approached the home of Thomas Jefferson. To fly over Monticello in a piece of transportation of that period was like stepping back into history.

After we landed, without an incident, we were all invited to a traditional champagne breakfast. Everyone was talking with excitement about what they had just experienced, and I had to thank my husband for setting up this trip of a lifetime that I would never forget. If fear had won, I would have regretted it forever.

Often you hear a senior citizen say, in the golden years of their lives, that they regretted the things they didn't do. Everything I did wasn't always the way I would have wanted it to be, but I have not regretted walking into new, sometimes scary, experiences. In short, I don't regret my life. And that's a pretty nice way to finish your life, which, by the way, isn't finished until God says it's finished.

A lot of people dread being in the air when a thunderstorm is brewing. True, you could experience some turbulence, but airlines are not out to take risks. The pilots are trained to give you a safe and enjoyable ride, from start to finish. But the weather can change, so we need to understand what happens if your trip should encounter a storm.

My first commercial airline flight was on our honeymoon. We were heading to Florida in August, as the sun was setting, a notorious time for storms to ignite... and they did. It really didn't affect our flight, but it did create an incredible light show out our window.

Admittedly, I was not a veteran flyer then, so I was a little nervous. Nelson assured me that there was nothing to worry about and we were in love, so I didn't worry or inquire further about flying in stormy weather.

Seventeen years later, having flown in small four-passenger planes, large wide-bodied planes, and crossed both oceans through many time zones, we were about to fly a Piper Warrior from Tucson to the Grand Canyon and back. Kirk was fourteen, and couldn't wait to get his pilot license, so Nelson allowed him to take the controls as we headed back to Tucson.

The engines are rather loud on small planes, so the only talking was between Nelson and Kirk through their headsets. I sat in the back, with my camera at the ready, as the sun was giving off an orange-red burst of color ahead of our plane.

Then I noticed the clouds beginning to darken on both sides of the horizon. I watched as a few bolts of lightning ripped from the base of the cloud to the ground. All of a sudden, my veteran status dissolved as fear began to pound in my ears. I tapped Nelson on the shoulder and shouted, "Shouldn't we turn around or land? Look at the storm clouds ahead. It looks serious."

In Nelson's usual unpanicked manner, he took the controls back from Kirk and assured me, once again, that everything was alright. We proceeded to fly through a broad opening between the two storms, as the dark foreboding cumulus clouds continued to rise higher and higher on both sides of us, and the lightning multiplied, with ground strikes to the city streets below. Amazingly, our little craft seemed like we were watching all this on a giant TV screen because we didn't experience any buffeting.

It wasn't until we were on the ground in Tucson that I was able to talk to Nelson about the fear of being struck by lightning. He explained that his commercial aircraft had been struck by lightning in the past, but the electricity just goes right through the fuselage and doesn't damage the aircraft. The phenomenon is called "Faraday Cage". In essence, the passengers are in a metal cage, the airplane, and the electrical charge flows over the outside of the aircraft. Wish I had known that before we started our flight, but I was glad to learn about it after the fact.

There are books that will help you to overcome your fear of flying. There are even classes that will take you slowly off the ground on short trips to overcome your white-knuckle approach to flying. I would strongly suggest that you look into one or both of these so that you can begin to experience new adventures above the clouds.

CHAPTER 7

Car Accidents

"Forget the former things, do not dwell on the
past."

(Isaiah 43:18 NIV)

Anyone reading this, who is at least twenty-five, has
probably been in a car accident as the driver or a passenger. It may have only been a fender-bender, but we
have all experienced an incident of one type or another.

Let me ask you, have you stopped traveling in a car?
If you did, that must be very confining for you. Unless
you live in the heart of a city, where you can walk to all
your shops and doctor's offices, you really put yourself

in a kind of self-made prison, haven't you? You've cut yourself off from family and friends.

While Jesus walked this earth, He had to take risks. True, there weren't any airplanes or cars to deal with, but there was still the possibility of drowning on the rough sea or trampled by a beast of burden, not to mention being mercilessly crucified. In short, living is risky. We can either choose to live or choose to be 100 percent safe by not traveling anywhere and wind up slipping in the shower.

I knew a man who said you should never have an accident if you practice defensive driving techniques. He said this after his wife came home with a crumpled fender. He sent her to a defensive driving class. I wasn't able to follow up on the two of them because we moved, but an accident is called an accident because you didn't plan it. Even with defensive driving classes, which are a good thing, you still may fall victim to an accident. The only difference is that you may be able to reduce the damages.

Helen Keller had been blind and deaf since she was a baby. Talk about risky. She took a risk just getting out of bed in the morning. If you couldn't see or hear or know if someone rearranged the furniture while you were sleeping, how risky would it be to just walk across the room?

Helen not only got out of bed thousands of times, but she finished college, wrote several books, worked to improve schools for the blind, and even learned to read lips with her fingertips.[24] She really lived for her eighty-seven years on this earth, overcoming the stigma of her time that said she should have been sent to an institution.[25] One of her quotes, which I love to repeat, reads, "...Avoiding danger is no safer in the long run, than outright exposure. Life is either a daring adventure, or nothing."[26]

Wow, I couldn't have said it better myself.

As I briefly mentioned earlier, I have been in seven car accidents, ranging from a simple fender-bender to totaling two cars. Some of them were not my fault, some of it had to deal with the car's design, the road conditions, the weather, and the part, none of us what to think about, is how we contributed to it. I have to confess that some of it was, unfortunately, my fault, at least in part.

I bring that up to help us not to think that everything that goes wrong is because of something someone else did... or didn't do. That's important to realize because if we don't see our part in the problem, then the problem is only going to come up again.

---

24 The Editors of Encyclopaedia Britannica, "Helen Keller," In Encyclopaedia Britannica, https://www.britannica.com/biography/Helen-Keller.

25 Ibid.

26 "Quote by Helen Keller," BrainyQuote, 2022, https://www.brainyquote.com/quotes/helen_keller_121787.

For example: If someone was in a car accident during a rainstorm, and the vehicle hit a guard rail, the driver might blame his car's damages on the weather. But if that driver had too many beers before sitting behind the wheel, he is ignoring his part in that accident, and it might wind up causing an even more serious outcome in the future. He really needs to take an honest look at the incident, be willing to accept his part in it, and even get some help with his drinking problem. (Yes, even beer and wine can cause you to slow down your reflexes and be a contributor to an accident. So, don't consume any alcoholic beverages when you intend to drive.)

I'm sure you're wondering what my accidents were about, and am I willing to see my contribution to the crash? Well, let's find out.

The first serious accident I had, was when I was twenty-six, married, and driving our only car, a Volvo station wagon, down a steep hill, with our two-year-old son, who was in a rather flimsy version of a child's car seat, in the seat behind me. There was a three-way intersection, at the bottom of the hill, with no light to direct the traffic. Both roads were two lanes, with a wide berm on the side of each road. It was also the beginning of rush hour, and the drivers were in a hurry to get home. The east and westbound traffic had the right-of-way, and so they had no problem getting through the intersection, until someone in front of them wanted to go up the hill. Traffic backed up, and cars began to go around each other onto the berm.

I would have turned around, but by that time, cars were backed up behind me, and several cars were making their way up the hill on my left. So, I waited until I was at the intersection. I turned on my left turn signal. I was now committed to cross in front of the oncoming cars to my left, as well as the car trying to go through the intersection on my right and the one speeding around that driver, so he could go up the hill.

Sound confusing? Feels like something bad is going to happen? Well, it did. A truck was coming from my left, over a rise, and even though I looked both ways, somehow, I missed seeing him. His truck tore up the front end of my vehicle, but thanks to the safety features in the Volvo, it never touched our son or me. However, it did total our car, and Kirk was crying. I wasn't seat belted, and my head hit the windshield. When I turned to check on my son, his headrest was completely bent backward. I was afraid he was injured, but he was only shaken up a bit and kept repeating, "Mommy bump, Mommy bump."

I trembled as I exited the car and assessed the damages. I was glad we were alive, and the truck driver was okay, but I was overwhelmed by all the issues that I now had before me. EMS workers took us to the hospital in an ambulance. The doctor said I had a concussion, and they wanted someone to look after me that night since I wasn't supposed to get into a deep sleep that I wouldn't be able to wake up from. Fortunately, my brother and nurse sister-in-law lived just a couple of miles up the road. They took Kirk and me back to their house, and Carrol kept watch over me all through the night.

I knew I had to call Nelson before he returned home from his trip. Explaining that our car had been totaled wasn't easy, but Nelson didn't get mad. He said we'd think of something and that he was glad we were both fine. That certainly was a relief to hear. However, I did have some serious doubts about whether I should ever drive again.

I had two minor accidents with my Mustang just before we were married. There were some external factors in both cases, but I had to admit, I made some bad decisions, too. So, when Nelson arrived home and a friend lent us his extra car until ours was repaired, I gave Nelson the right to tear up my driver's license. I didn't want to be responsible for any more issues that could hurt our family or pocketbook.

Sometimes, during our trials, our loved ones let us down. That's unfortunate because that's when we need them the most. While Nelson was a man of few words, he never flattered me or yelled at me. In fact, I had often wished he would yell just so we could clear the air. But on this day, he said just the right thing. He assured me that accidents happen and that fear shouldn't dictate whether I drive or not. While he wanted me to be careful and to remember to wear my seatbelt, he didn't berate me or shout me down.

Gotta love him.

In time, the mechanics restored our Volvo so it could be back on the road. I went back to driving around the airport area, and within two years, we decided to move to the country with, our then, two children.

We bought eight acres up against tracts of beautiful game lands in northwestern Pennsylvania. Since we now needed two cars, Nelson and I decided to look for an inexpensive used car. We found a used VW that was only $800. The windshield wipers didn't work very well, but the car ran okay, and I would have something to fall back on whenever I needed transportation.

My used VW seemed to be working well for me until one day in August 1978, when Kimberly was five and Kirk was nine. Nelson was home and needed to take his car to the dealer to fix the air conditioner. We all planned to drive into Meadville, about forty-five minutes away, and get some shopping done while the dealer worked on Nelson's car.

Nelson left our property first with Kirk, and I followed with Kim. Before we reached the main county road, we had, what some folks would call, a gully washer. I lost sight of Nelson's car as I tried to see through the flood of rain that blanketed my windshield. Suddenly, the rain stopped, Nelson was out of sight, and I turned on the radio to relax. Without any warning, I lost control of my steering. The engine in the VW was in the back, so the car had no weight to keep the front tires on the road as I drove into a stream of water flowing over the oily asphalt. I began to hydroplane.

Even though I had always insisted that the children had to be seat belted, Kim would frequently unbuckle her belt so that she could look out the window. Also, I wasn't the best example because I often failed to wear my seat belt. When another VW approached us in the opposite direction, neither of us was belted in. I crossed the center line, and we hit nearly head-on.

Kim died instantly, and I was tossed around inside the car until I landed on the front floorboard. The ambulance driver rushed me to the hospital, where they discovered I had a shattered hip, two fractured vertebrae, two teeth had splintered, exposing the nerve, all my organs were bleeding internally, and I had lacerations and bruises over my entire body. The doctor had to stitch up my chin because my jaw bone was exposed.

A lot of my friends couldn't understand why God would allow this to happen to us. But I gradually woke up to the fact that our trials are our own. Others can pray for us and send us their sympathy, but please don't try to figure out what God is doing in someone else's life.

Of course, in the beginning of my two-month recovery in the hospital, I was just trying to survive. But later, I tried to put all the pieces together and make a reasonable decision as to how to face my future without our daughter. I'll cover more about the loss of a child in the next chapter. Because every trial has a lesson at the end of it, even if you can't understand it for months or years, let's see what we can learn from those two major accidents that I was in:

- We weren't seat belted. Our family could have avoided a lot of pain, sorrow, and doctor's bills if we had been. I ALWAYS wear a seatbelt now.
- In both cases, we did not have an age-appropriate car seat for our children, partly due to the fact that they hadn't made the sturdy ones they have available today. Be sure to buy a well-made car seat for your children and know-how and where to secure it in your car. The police can help you with that.
- If you have a choice, find the safest route to where you are going, even though this may cost you some extra time to get there. You may also want to pick a better hour of the day to travel.
- When you are buying a used car, remember the precious cargo it is carrying, namely your loved ones. Look up safety facts for that make of car

and the specific report on that particular car's history before purchasing it.

- Even though you may be traveling at the speed limit, still take weather conditions into account, and slow down when necessary. While heavy rain may not affect the road you are on, it may be flooding on another piece of the highway, so slow down.

- Reschedule an event, rather than rushing to something or going through bad weather to get there. Even canceling is better than having an accident.

Yes, car accidents do occur more frequently than any other form of travel, partly because there are so many cars and trucks on our highways. The majority are either fender-benders or cause minor injuries, and many of those accidents could have been prevented.

Cars and buses, as well as our large trucks, are essential to our lives today. Even the Amish, who don't own cars, find the need to ask for a ride to some events that are too far away for them to go to by horse and buggy.

While I'm sure Jesus enjoyed the exercise and inspiration of walking down roads as He visited with His friends and followers, He also used a boat or donkey on occasion. Do you think He would have driven a car if it had been invented back then?

Don't let a past accident stop you from visiting friends or helping others. Think of the many trips you have made with no incidents, and think of the pleasure you had going out to dinner or taking a family trip across the country.

CHAPTER 8

Loss of Your Child

My comfort in my suffering is this: Your
promise preserves my life.

(Psalm 119:50 NIV)

I have often heard that the greatest loss is the loss of
your child. Kim's death left a hole in all of us that never
really healed. Time does heal a little, but she is still a
part of us, and especially me, the one who carried her
for nine months and nursed her for over a year.

I had to live with the fact that I was driving the car
that took her life. Guilt and all the *what-ifs* haunted me.
What if Kim had gone with Nelson and not me? What

if we started our journey sooner? What if I had slowed down more?

There had been a witness to the crash, and that witness, along with the police report, did not site me with reckless driving. The police did cite me as the cause of the crash because I hydroplaned and went over the centerline. So, in essence, according to the law, I was responsible for all the injuries that followed, including the death of our daughter and the hospitalization of the woman in the other car.

I managed to mentally accept a part of the tragedy; after all, I was driving. But I couldn't bear all of the blame. Fortunately, the Christian woman in the other car called from her hospital bed to say that she was so sorry for my loss and that she didn't blame me because it was, in fact, an accident. That was amazing to hear from this woman, who had to have a pin put in her ankle, and she remained in the hospital for almost three months.

I was also surprised by the question my unmarried aunt presented me with when she came to visit me in the hospital. "Are you sorry you had her?"

"What did you say?"

"I just wondered, after all the pain of losing your daughter, are you sorry you had her?"

Wow, that explained a lot of things. My aunt had lost her father when she was only seven. She lost her brother, who died on a submarine in WWII, and she was very close to him. Each of her many fiancés left her when she couldn't commit to marriage. She was a very attractive woman, but I had often wondered why, after being engaged to several men, she never decided to marry, and now I knew.

My aunt was afraid to lose someone that she loved. If she never committed to anyone, then she couldn't get hurt. And yet, she was hurting herself. She was painfully lonely. Going on dates and collecting engagement rings didn't end her loneliness.

I finally was able to answer her. "No, I am not sorry I had Kimberly. She is forever a part of my life; her smiles are indelibly etched into my memory. And I know I will see her again. I'm sorry she isn't here now, but no, I would never dream of leaving her out of my life, even after feeling the pain of her loss."

Yes, I said all of that from a face filled with bruises and stitches and a mouth full of shattered teeth.

After I arrived home from the hospital, I was equally amazed to receive a phone call from our insurance company. They wanted to know if Nelson, my husband, the father of our children, was going to sue me for the death of our daughter? I couldn't believe it. They explained that many spouses would sue their partner if they felt they were responsible for the death of their child. Thankfully, that was the furthest thing from Nelson's mind. I was also glad I had read a book titled *The Bereaved Parent* while I was recuperating. It said that over 80 percent of marriages break up after the death of their child. One bereaved parent might turn to alcohol, the other might become isolated and depressed, or one may turn into a workaholic, so they don't have to think about their loss. I could see how that could dissolve a marriage, but I was determined that we would stay together, all three of us.

I recalled how one teacher friend of mine had handled the loss of her one daughter. She turned their home into a shrine. Pictures of her first child decorated her home, including a large portrait over their fireplace, while her other daughter seemed to be forgotten. In fact, I didn't know she had another daughter.

I was determined not to immortalize Kim. I asked Kirk if he was okay with me hanging some pictures of Kim on the wall in our rec room. He was fine with that, and I felt good about it, too. I didn't want to forget her nor make her the center of everything we did.

The other things that helped me get through it all, mentally, were that Kim hadn't suffered and wasn't recovering from her injuries in another wing of the hospital. She was at peace. Also, it was comforting to know that I had spent a lot of time with our daughter. She loved standing near my sewing machine while I constructed a floppy dog and made outfits for her *Baby, Baby* doll.

She helped me by hanging up our socks on a wire that supported our grapevine while I hung the rest of our laundry on the higher clothesline next to our house. Our family went to Hawaii, Disney World, and Alaska, and she was crowned *Little Miss Queen of Townville* the year before she died. In fact, she had just given up her crown to another little girl the week before the accident.

At the end of that homecoming event in Townville, Kim was slowly walking back to our car with me. She just wasn't her usual bubbly self. I sensed that she was sad that she had given up her crown, the royal cape, and the bouquet of flowers to the other little girl, as she had rehearsed days before. She agreed, that was part of it, but she was happy that Stacey won because she had already met her and was looking forward to playing with her again in kindergarten that September.

Something inspired me to say, "You know, Kim, one day you will receive a crown that no one will take from you when you are in heaven."

She smiled up at me as she began to skip to the car. It seemed prophetic that those were the words I chose to say a week before she was gone from me.

Since I wasn't able to attend her funeral, I found comfort in my deep belief in the resurrection. I no longer just talk about the resurrection of the dead, but I was now walking in that truth. We *would* meet again.

Two real blessings for me were my husband and son. Nelson didn't blame me. In fact, he was sorry that he hadn't bought me a safer car. I reminded him that we had both agreed on the purchase of that car, but he still felt a certain responsibility for the tragedy, as did I.

Nelson was even able to look at me with all my stitches, bruises, and matted hair and say, "You're beautiful!" For a man who didn't say much, he certainly said the right thing then. I knew it was love talking and not his eyesight, but that made it even more special.

Kirk never showed any tears. Knowing he had been with his dad and wasn't able to break down with the people who took care of him while Nelson worked, I told him it was all right to cry. He said, "There's nothing to cry about. Kim isn't hurting, and you're getting better." That pretty much summed it up.

One day, when Kirk and Nelson were doing a little project together from a Bible workbook, Kirk drew a shield that represented our family. It had a sun on one corner, the four of us together in another corner, and the word, strength, written diagonally across the entire shield. Wow, was that how he saw our family, with his mom flat on her back, in traction, in the hospital? God was blessing us in spite of the circumstances.

That's rather interesting since I often laid alone in my hospital bed, whispering, "God, where are you?" I couldn't imagine that a born-again Christian would be going through so much mental and physical pain. And yet, I always tried to encourage my despondent visitors with the very real promises of God and my deep belief in seeing our daughter again. I told everyone how blessed Kim was to have experienced so much in her short time on this earth... and then... when I was alone... I'd again ask, "Where are you, God?"

It took me a while to realize that He was in the midst of my nightmare. Not torturing me, but reassuring me with His Word that He put in my own mouth. God surrounded me with my family and friends. I slowly realized that there were lessons to be learned from this trial that went beyond seatbelts and the choice of my next car. I was learning to be more compassionate about other people's trials, not judging them but embracing them.

After I was released from the hospital, I was on crutches and about fifty pounds lighter. My mother and retired father came to stay with us until I felt I could manage on my own. My mother was a good cook, so she tried to please me with all my favorite foods. Pot roasts, mashed potatoes and gravy, spaghetti, and homemade pies, were the menu of the day.

Suddenly, I was having symptoms of the flu. I was throwing up and suffering from extreme bouts of diarrhea. By the time Nelson arrived home, we thanked my folks and asked them to leave, so Nelson could take me to be checked out by the doctor.

Dr. Kirkpatrick said I was Jaundice. He thought I had created some gallstones while lying flat in bed for two months. He was right. So, I was back in the hospital and concerned that our son would be devastated. Like his dad, he seemed to be managing amazingly well. Over time, I discovered that he had suffered quietly, and I would say to anyone who has lost a child and has other children to encourage the other child to talk about their concerns, even if they don't want to, and even find counseling so that issues can be dealt with before they grow bigger.

As it happened, we were to go to Arizona in a week, with our friends, as a part of our church's convention, and there I was, back in the hospital. I told Nelson to cancel our plans. But then... as so often God has a way of butting into our lives, I met a woman I had never met before. She was in a bed in another part of the hospital. She attended a different branch of our church and had heard of our car accident.

When I entered her room, she offered me her condolences and then said, "Where will you be going for this year's convention? My family will be going to Mt. Pocono this weekend."

I couldn't believe that this woman, on a ventilator, with asthma, would consider traveling to frosty Mt. Poconos in late Autumn. As I stood there, balancing on my crutches, I was about to say, "Well, we're not going," but encouraged by her enthusiasm, I instead said, "To Arizona."

Later that day, when Nelson came to the hospital to tell me he had canceled our reservations, I said, "Call them back and set them up again because we're going."

My very reluctant doctor, who wanted me to get my gall bladder out, right away, approved the discharge after I promised him I would keep to a strict diet and I'd see him when we got back. It was a bit risky, I suppose, looking back on my decision now, and I wouldn't recommend that you do what I did, but my point is that we can't let fear control us.

Reuniting with my friends and experiencing the splendor of the Grand Canyon for the first time together as a new family of three was a very healing time for me. Even though it was difficult to get around in a wheelchair and crutches and restaurants weren't as exciting as they had been when I could only eat a baked potato and a salad with vinegar and oil dressing followed by a tablespoon of lecithin granules for the entire week, but I don't regret my decision.

As much as I wanted to be healed instantly, that two-month stay in the hospital taught me a lot about patience, love, and God's grace. For three months, my life was a whirlwind of doctors, people, travel, and rehab... and then came the next hurdle.

The chill of Autumn had blanketed our little farm. We had to return to some new kind of normalcy without the sunshine of our perky young daughter. I hadn't actually had time to mourn or think. But now, as Kirk prepared to go back to school and Nelson drove off to work... I was alone.

I limped around the house, got on a coat, and fed the kittens, chickens, and our dog, Heidi, and then I came back in the front door to tackle the one room I had avoided, Kim's room. I had painted it a golden yellow and made her bedspread and curtains out of colorful bedsheets that were adorned with kittens and hearts. Her favorite stuffed toys were on the bed, and her musical jewelry box sat on the dresser under the window.

I only cried once about Kim's death while I was in the hospital. I shed a deluge of tears that day, and then it stopped. I thought the tears were over.

I don't cry easily, but now I was standing in the reality of the death of our little girl. Her room stored her giggles, her pouts, her love, and her girlishness. I was glad that Nelson didn't discard everything. I asked him not to, even though he wanted to spare me.

I looked through her pastel clothes in her closet, punctuated with bows, hearts, and ruffles. I perused her precious collection of stones and buttons as I sat down on her bed and began to rock her favorite teddy bear. "Lullaby and good night, go to sleep..." the words turned into sobs. Tears flowed from my eyes as I rocked and sang for what seemed like an hour.

Then, it was as if a lightning bolt hit me. I sat up straight and remembered a movie I saw called *The Snake*

Pit. It depicted a turn-of-the-century mental hospital that had the severest patients marching around on the floor beneath a balcony, hence the name, the snake pit. It was like they weren't people at all but snakes thrashing in a hole in the ground. One lady stood out because she was just calmly sitting in a rocking chair, holding a baby doll, and singing lullabies.

"Dear God, that's me!"

I immediately dried my tears, laid out some boxes on the floor, and began to separate Kimberly's belongings into several categories. One box was for my friend Carol's girls, and one was for Goodwill. I divided up her toys among some of her friends and kept one small box just for me to open once in a while to remember her by.

Mourning is different for everyone. But there does have to be an end to it, eventually. You can't spend your life crying over the loss of a child, a parent, or a spouse. If that sounds cold, it isn't. Life is for living. You can't live in pity or a state of mourning.

Ecclesiastes 3:1–8 says...

> To everything, there is a season,
> A time to every purpose under heaven:
> A time to be born,
> A time to die (...)
> A time to weep,
> And a time to laugh;

A time to mourn,

And a time to dance...

(NKJV)

Steven Spielberg made a TV series titled, *Into the West*. As the wagon train was moving west, the group of pioneers encountered a storm with the resultant stampede of their livestock. In the course of the pandemonium, a child was killed. The mother wanted to remain on the open prairie, next to the grave of her child. After several men convinced her to change her mind, she climbed back on their wagon with her other child and husband, and they continued their long trek to California. Just a few days after the death of that child, those same pioneers had a square dance and were singing. So, why did I take the time to tell this story? One of the narrator's lines of the story was, "grief was a luxury that none of us could afford."[27]

Did you ever think that your tears and sadness during the mourning period that we all acknowledge as normal is a luxury? If you stop to think about the ongoing hardships the pioneers had to face every day, even every hour of every day—from Indians to wagons breaking down, to illnesses, to seemingly impassable

---

27 Robert Dornhelm, Simon Wincer, Sergio Mimica-Gezzan, Michael W. Watkins, Timothy Van Patten, and Jeremy Podeswa, Into the West - Part 2 (Manifest Destiny), YouTube, 2005 https://www.youtube.com/watch?v=GCnayRFj-2M.

mountain ranges, they really didn't have the *luxury* to stop and cry about it.

I'm not saying we shouldn't cry. I'm just saying we have to stop and allow life to come pouring back into us. To really live your life the way God wants you to, you must move beyond sorrow.

While I was still on my crutches, an older lady in our small town, whom I had never met before, called me to say she had a gift for me. Nelson and I went to her house and found that she had obtained an 8" x 10" picture of our daughter from the local newspaper on the day she gave up her crown.

The woman had several surgeries in the past year. Her friends couldn't understand why she was having so many problems because she was a kind and devoted Christian woman who should have been blessed with good health. Her response was a gift that I will never forget. She said, "Why not me? We all go through difficult trials, but as a Christian, I should be an example of how to deal with difficulties and not be bitter or defeated." Since then, I have never asked God, why me? I have always asked God to make me strong enough to handle whatever comes my way.

Thirty years later, I began reviewing everything that had come out of that overwhelming tragedy, and I discovered many precious lessons that I learned, which I put into another book I wrote, titled: *Treasures from the Wreckage*.

One of those lessons was to be thankful I had Kirk to care for. He gave me a purpose. And something that, for me, disproves the long-held opinion that the worst loss is that of your child... is when I contemplated what I would have done without my husband. It is why married couples need to make their marriages the best they can be. I needed Nelson more than ever. He was there at Kim's birth, he cared for Kirk while I was incapacitated, he took care of all the necessary funeral preparations that we had not anticipated in our mid-thirties... and he loved me.

While the loss of a child means the loss of all the dreams you have for them and the joy you gain from watching them grow, the loss of a good husband or wife is incalculable, as I learned then and in the years to come.

CHAPTER 9

Lawsuits

He delivers me from my enemies. You also lift
me up above those who rise against me; You
have delivered me from the violent man.

(Psalm 18:48 NKJV)

Unless you are in big business or have a large profile, most of us never expect to deal with a lawyer over a lawsuit that has been brought against us. We just go about our everyday ups and downs, cleaning up spilled milk or paying our ever-increasing bills.

But if you have been in a car accident that injures another person or property, you better be insured and pray that the company you're with has a good lawyer to defend you. Even though the lady in the other car that I hit head-on was covered by our insurance company and had all her incurred bills paid at the time, she had two years to file a lawsuit for more money.

Almost to the day, two years after the accident, in 1980, a police officer drove up our long gravel driveway in his police car. I came out of our house to inquire what he needed.

"Are you Donna Trickett?" he asked in a very official manner.

"Yes."

"This is for you." He handed me a summons that I was being sued and would need to show up in court.

I held that court order in my trembling hand as I watched the officer return to his car and drive away. Tears began to blur my vision. I was frozen in fear. We were just beginning to think that we could put that awful day behind us and get on with our lives when I now had to face a lawsuit. As I went back to the house, eleven-year-old Kirk saw that I was crying. He asked, "What's wrong, Mom? What did the policeman want?"

"I'll be fine, Kirk. Just give me a few minutes. I've just been served papers that I need to go to court about a lawsuit pertaining to the car accident in 1978."

It was Autumn, and we were preparing to go to our church's convention in England in a few weeks. We had never flown abroad, so it was going to be a very unique and educational experience for us. All of a sudden, my joy turned to dread as I anticipated us canceling all our plans and spending weeks entangled in this lawsuit.

Nelson and I called our insurance company to explain the situation and find out what our options were. They said since it was for a religious observation, we could go out of the country, but we would have to give them all our contacts and itinerary, so they could call us back at a moment's notice. They had lawyers that would represent us, but if the court required our presence, we needed to show up within twenty-four hours. It definitely put a pressure on our celebration, but of course, we agreed.

In 1980, we didn't have cell phones. So, we had to call back to our insurance company on British payphones every few hours to see how things were progressing and let them know where we were.

Back then, overseas phone calls were not easy to make. First, we had to deal with the time zone differences. Then, we had to drop in coins we weren't familiar with to pay the exact change required for the long-distance call. Any busy signal or being put on hold only made matters more stressful. This was to be a trip that inspired us to learn more about the Bible and meet with other brethren from around the world, and not worry about how many shillings were in our pockets for the next phone call.

Despite the distraction of the lawsuit, we managed to meet fellow Christians from many countries, discover new facts about the Isle of Man, my family's origin, and be inspired by many of the sermons that we heard. We had managed to separate the lawsuit from our Christian pursuit, at least between phone calls.

Then, one morning, as we were sitting down to breakfast with others who were staying at our hotel, a waitress delivered a letter to me. It was a message from our insurance company saying they had settled the lawsuit. We could relax and enjoy the rest of our trip.

Our burden was lifted. I felt so relieved that I wanted to burst into song. Instead, we said an additional prayer at that meal to thank God for taking care of the problem and to ask Him to help the woman who had brought the lawsuit against us.

That wasn't just a nice gesture on our part, but I truly meant it. She was a beautician and a single mom who had to be on her feet a lot, and then she found herself injured in this accident. I knew she meant well when she called me from her hospital bed. I knew she wasn't being malicious when I was served with those papers. She was probably struggling months after the accident; I know I was. I had a limp and some limitations that never really went away. So, I wanted her to receive whatever was fair, but I was also very glad that it was finally settled.

One year later, Kirk was having more and more problems with allergies to many of the items found on our mini-farm, like cottonwood trees, cats, and hay. He was developing asthma, so we moved back to a less rural setting, a bit closer to Nelson's work. We found a house near Youngstown that had a pond and a few acres of mowed lawn. Other kids were just across the street, and we no longer had to deal with the dust that kicked up from our dirt road when a car or truck went by.

Kirk was starting seventh grade. A difficult time for any young teen to walk into, but he was smart, and he quickly made friends with some of the young boys on our street. Unfortunately, his health problems were beginning to emerge again, even though we had moved away from the majority of his allergens. Then, when he came home from school, having been hit in the head with a chunk of ice, I confronted the principal. He claimed he couldn't do anything about the problem, but the school would arrange for a tutor while he recovered.

Nelson and I agreed that the loss of his sister just three years earlier, a new school, allergies, and now the violence erupting on the bus and school grounds were just too much. We began to look at alternatives.

I had a teaching certificate, and homeschoolers were beginning to organize, even though, in most states, and Ohio was one of them, it was still illegal to homeschool. Nevertheless, again, I approached the principal to see if

I could teach our son at home for one year, just until he could cope better with all his issues.

The principal immediately stopped the tutor (who was still a student in college, herself) and threatened not to pass him from seventh grade unless he returned to school immediately. I said I would check with our doctor, and they sent me to the local school superintendent and then to the county school superintendent, who informed me that I might be in a lot of trouble if Kirk wasn't back in school within the week.

While our doctor felt he needed to be home for now because he was thriving health-wise, the superintendent said they would test him with their doctor and psychologist, suggesting that they felt he might have psychological issues. Kirk was an "A" student who made friends easily and did not get in fights, and the school system wanted to find a reason that would require him to attend their public school.

Having taught in the public schools and knowing how a psychologist can read into test results in any number of ways, I refused their request and said we would obtain a psychologist from another district to test him.

She did, and he tested out of high school with an IQ of 145, and socially, she found that Kirk was well adjusted and highly gifted. When she heard we were contemplating homeschooling and travel due to my husband's job, she felt it was an excellent choice for him because it would keep him stimulated. She put all of that information in her written report.

At the time, there were cases where homeschoolers were being arrested. Moms were physically taken to jail, and the child was put in foster care until the parent would recant. I certainly didn't want to add any more trauma to our son or go to jail, but the school was giving me no alternative but to fight back legally.

Now, you may be wondering why I am saying "I" instead of "we," meaning Nelson and me? My husband was totally backing me, but it was the mother who was targeted because moms were normally the ones at home, teaching the child. And in our case, Nelson's job took him away for days at a time, so phone calls, legal responses, and teaching Kirk were mostly my responsibility. Thus, I would be the one persecuted.

I found a lawyer in Cleveland who worked with the homeschooling issue. He was in a wheelchair, which actually worked to our advantage because the small courthouse was not able to accommodate him with a ramp. That put the school officials on the defense, as they scrambled to find a building with a room on the first floor, so we could meet with an assistant district attorney, the county school superintendent, and the truant officer to settle this issue once and for all.

If you're wondering where I got the hutzpah to stand up to such a fortress, I can only say that God had been working in me, bringing me up to this place through all the trials I had already come through. After Kim's death, there just didn't seem to be a lot of things to intimidate me anymore. Being sure our son's health and education were being taken care of properly became a major purpose for me.

I was scared when we met in the annex next to the courthouse. In fact, my knees were shaking under the table, but I pulled out my attaché, proposed curriculum, my college diploma, and my trembling courage and proceeded to present our case. I surprised myself, and I think I even surprised my husband. That's what you can do if you don't run from your trials or think it's too big for you and give up. With each triumph, you become less fearful and more battle-ready for whatever the future holds.

While our lawyer was in attendance, he said nothing. He had already couched me all the way down from Cleveland on the Attorney General's ruling and criteria for a private school, which was how a homeschool was categorized. In the end, we became the first approved homeschool in Columbiana County, Ohio, which made us one of the pioneers that helped open up homeschooling to not only Ohio but America.

Wow, who knew? With God on your side, you can do anything.

By the way, if you think I became an over-protective mom to our son, I can only add that I drove him to the small, local airport in our town to learn to fly a small plane, before he could drive a car when he was only fifteen. And I encouraged him to participate in all the sporting events our church had created for our teenagers, from track to basketball. I wanted him to experience a full life, not a sheltered one.

CHAPTER 10

Going Broke

Keep your lives free from the love of money
and be content with what you have, because
God has said, "Never will I leave you: never
will I forsake you."

(Hebrews 13:5 NIV)

Kirk received his high school diploma in the mail
from the local high school. He went on to college in Texas and graduated from UT in 1990 with honors and a
bachelor's degree in computers. He met his future wife,
Sabrina, in Texas, and they were married that same
year.

Kirk and Sabrina eventually moved back to Ohio, where he began working for the State of Ohio in the up-and-coming field known as IT. Then, as the year 1999 began to come to an end, an enormous fear arose that would threaten everyone, whether you owned a computer or not.

The new threat was called: "Y2K," meaning the "Year 2000". Now that Y2K is behind us, you may have forgotten how terrifying it was, or you may not have been born yet. So, let me explain.

When personal computers were first brought to the marketplace in 1975, they were programmed for the 1900s. In other words, all that binary coding was not ready to roll into the year 2000. Computer experts were predicting that all the computers in the world would shut down at midnight on December 31, 1999. We had progressed so quickly, from a Commodore 64K in the 1980s, to the more sophisticated Apple computer, with an entirely new vocabulary of terms, such as ROM, RAM, cursor, gigabytes, motherboard, Google, Microsoft, Windows, etc. While most of us were grappling with the new words, IT workers, like our son, were having to struggle with the possible collapse of our economy.

People were afraid the stock market would collapse, and we wouldn't be able to do business because everyone, from our banks to our grocery stores, required the use of the computer. We knew what it was like to have a computer crash for a few hours when you were trying to retrieve important information, but what if *all* the computers in the world couldn't digest the new 2000 code?

Financial advisors and even some ministers were warning people to prepare for an economic collapse. Much like the '50s, when people panicked and built expensive bomb shelters, people were panicking now, but they weren't building bomb shelters.

My husband and I listened to our neighbors, feeling like the end of the world was about to happen. They were hoarding preserved foods and water and buying generators to provide electricity if the electric companies couldn't function. Some were buying gold because that's what you do when you think America's economy will fail.

Nelson and I began to consider having an informational meeting in our small community. We asked if we could use our town hall to have the meeting and invite speakers to inform the attendees of exactly what Y2K meant. That would, we hoped, dispel many of the disturbing predictions that were terrorizing our neighborhood and nation.

To be fair, I asked speakers from both factions to present their cases. One woman told us that she stored about a year's worth of food and water in her basement. She said she wanted to survive any shortages that might come from the hoarding that was inevitable. She didn't equate that she, herself, had become a super hoarder. And she didn't look ahead to the fact that her very survival during such a disaster would make her a target for anyone who wanted to feed their family. I hoped it would open the eyes of any members of the audience who contemplated doing the same by listening to her, without saying that it was a bad idea.

The meeting turned out to be a kind of *show and tell* method of teaching, rather than a lecture. I guess it helped, some, but the fear continued until midnight, as the clock ticked into the new year, January 1, 2000, when all the lights did **not** go out, Y2K proved to be highly exaggerated. Although our son did say that it wasn't totally problem-free, in the end, the issues weren't as gigantic as the news media had predicted.

As soon as people saw that the world was still chugging along, with computers working at faster and faster speeds, they relaxed—I kind of wonder what the lady did with a year's worth of preserved foods. Personally, I prefer a fresh steak and potato dinner over a dehydrated pouch of dried beef.

Nelson and I really weren't worried about it. A little concerned, but not enough to stop the sale of our home and the purchase of a new home, just as the calendar was transitioning into the new year. We didn't do it to prove that we weren't afraid; we just felt that, since Nelson had retired, we needed to move on and find a property that would cover all of our bases. Enough room for guests, located near a playground where future grandchildren could play, and not a huge lawn to maintain.

Since we knew enough of our Bible to realize that Y2K might be a bump in our road, it wasn't going to be the end of the world. There were too many things that needed to happen first. So, we went where few would venture; when the clock struck midnight, we held two mortgages. Within a week, we closed on our old house, but for a brief moment, we took a deep breath and watched the hour-hand move to the top of the clock.

Were we foolish? Maybe. But we did have a beautiful home for a while that did serve us very well and allowed us to help others. Had we been controlled by fear, we would have missed out on a wonderful chapter in our lives.

I do believe that God blesses us, often in some of our weaker moments, when we don't make the best decisions because He sees what our motivation is, or He sees a valuable lesson that we can learn from our mistakes.

Mother Teresa was once quoted to say: "We fear the future because we are wasting today."[28]

Think about that. How much time is wasted during all the fears we have that could have been spent fulfilling our family's dreams, helping someone, finding so-

---

28 "104 Mother Teresa Quotes on Giving & Kindness (LOVE)," Gracious Quotes, 2022, https://graciousquotes.com/mother-teresa/.

lutions, or just enjoying our family rather than escalating our anxieties?

With all the uncertainty in the world, it is hard to be confident in anything. We hear the stories of the Stock Market Crash of 1929 and the resultant Great Depression, and it's difficult to know what to do with one's money.

Nelson had taken an early retirement package from the airline in 1994 and was given a lump sum, which we needed to invest in order to live off of it for the rest of our lives. Since we were still in our '50s, we needed to be wise with our money. The problem was we had never invested in anything before, so we really didn't have a clue as to what would be the best place to put nearly a million dollars. If you're not familiar with financial planning, you might think that you could just put it in the bank and live off of that sum for a long, long time. The truth is, inflation starts shrinking your savings, even with some monthly interest, so the wise steward seeks wise counsel.

One of our other problems was we only knew one financial advisor, personally. He was a longtime friend. It seemed more sensible to go with someone we knew than with some big corporation handling our money. We invested our money with our friend when the stock market was doing well. Even with our monthly withdrawals, the IRA grew to over a million dollars in the year 2000.

When I was growing up, the only millionaires I knew of were John D. Rockefeller and Andrew Carnegie. Now we were on our way to becoming multimillionaires, right?

First of all, it's important to realize that investing in the stock market is risky. It can go up, but it can also go down, and if your only income is from your investments, it can be a disaster. We were also trying to start a little business that we both worked together to supplement our income. But, in all honesty, neither of us was business-minded. We worked with children as entertainers, but it was more of a hobby than a business since we spent more on inventory than we made. So, if you do want to supplement your income with a business, be sure you know what you're doing and that you establish the business before you retire.

Six years later, we felt rather secure and wanted to find a larger home than our two-bedroom ranch, with less yard to maintain instead of our two acres with a pond. So, we purchased the largest home we had ever owned, thinking it would allow us to have a live-in nurse if we needed it and still have an extra room for family to stay over. As I mentioned earlier, we purchased it in January of 2000.

One year later, after 9–11, the stock market dropped drastically, and we were losing large chunks of money every month. Our friend/advisor was fighting cancer and having marital problems, so we had no idea where to turn. The majority of financial advisors suggested that investors should wait; the market would turn. So, we waited... and waited... and waited. In less than two years, we almost lost everything. At the very end, we realized that we could have put the investment into cash, but it was too late.

Due to the large mortgage on our beautiful new home, we had to sell it and move to something more affordable. At that same time, Kirk and Sabrina had planned to adopt an older child, so we moved closer to them. The prospect of becoming grandparents made our financial losses less painful. We also found another financial advisor. Fortunately, we had learned a lot about finances and the stock market in those nine years since Nelson retired.

One thing we did right was we had committed to tithing to the church at the very beginning of our marriage. When the money was going down, it was difficult to give 10 percent, but Nelson always paid that first before paying anything else, and we always had enough at the end of each month. It's the only explanation I have of how we got through that recession and others that followed.

We quickly stopped thinking like millionaires and began to be more thankful and content with what we had. To quote my mother, as she was reduced to one room in a nursing home, "It's all I need."

Our son ran into some financial issues over the health care cost of one of their adopted children. They wound up declaring Chapter 13 Bankruptcy. It took a few years, but they worked through it, paid off their debts, was cleared of the bankruptcy, and rebuilt their credit score.

There's nothing shameful about declaring bankruptcy. It is a legal option, and it has been used by many entrepreneurs who found their debt exceeding their income. Even God had instituted a *Year of Jubilee* that forgave a person's debt and helped him get back on his feet again, but, unfortunately, it isn't practiced today. So, we have the option of declaring bankruptcy instead.

The real problem is not taking responsibility for your debt.

To quote Socrates, from 499 B.C., "He is richest who is content with the least, for content is the wealth of nature."[29] With all the things available to us, with just the swipe of a credit card, it's a good quote to remember.

---

29 "Quote by Socrates," BrainyQuote, 2022, https://www.brainyquote.com/quotes/socrates_163092.

CHAPTER 11

Terrorists

You will hear of wars and rumors of wars, but
see to it that you are not alarmed. Such things
must happen, but the end is still to come.

(Matthew 24:6 NIV)

If you remember 9–11–2001, you experienced a fear
of terrorism that has never gone away. When two commercial jets hit the twin towers in New York, and another struck the Pentagon in Washington, D.C., our entire
world changed in just a matter of hours.

I was busy at my computer that morning in the little
town of Grove City, just outside of Columbus, Ohio. I

was irritated that an entire chapter I hadn't saved had disappeared from the monitor as I was writing my first book. I didn't want to call our son for help until he was finished with his job at the state capitol when the phone rang. It was Kirk.

I felt relieved that God had answered my prayer as I said, "Oh, Kirk, good, I wanted to call you, but..."

Kirk interrupted, "Mom, are you sitting down?"

"Yes. Why?" I answered with concern about the seriousness in his voice.

"We are under a terrorist attack. The Twin Towers in New York and the Pentagon were attacked by commercial planes and another plane just went down in Pennsylvania after it took off from Cleveland. They are evacuating our building for fear that there may be more planes ready to attack our state capitals."

I was in shock. "Oh, God, no!" I finally responded.

"I wondered if we could meet somewhere for dinner? Just to talk."

"Yeah, sure. Ahhhh... What about Zanesville? We could meet at the Olive Garden Restaurant."

"Sounds good. How about six o'clock?"

"Fine."

Nelson was down the road at our church doing some yardwork. As soon as he came in the door, I told him the news, and we sat down to watch the horrifying footage of that morning played over and over again on all the channels. It left us numb. Where do we go from here? How was it going to affect our country? Were we at war?

As we headed out to the restaurant at about five that evening, it was eerie. There were hardly any cars on the main thoroughfares at rush hour. There were no contrails in the sky from normal airline traffic over our city. There were hardly any sounds of life that usually were heard at the end of the day.

President George W. Bush had ordered all planes grounded, including those coming into the United States from other countries. Air traffic controllers had to land hundreds of large aircraft coming from overseas at small airports outside of the United States' territory.

Only one other couple showed up at the restaurant. We did more talking than eating that night. Exchanging words of shaky encouragement, we parted and began a new life in a new world full of anxiety over safety. The government even created a new security group at our airports after that day, called the Transportation Security Administration (TSA).

X-ray machines were no longer adequate to ensure a passenger's safety and the safety of our nation. We now had pat-downs, body x-rays, and we were even asked to remove our shoes and belts before going through the standard metal detectors.

Fear and panic had taken over our nation. Airports were nearly empty. Soldiers were being called up to go to the middle east to retaliate against the terrorists.

In October, just a few weeks after the attack, Kirk was asked, by his boss, to fly to Florida for a special training class. He enquired if we would like to join him there, during one of his days off, so we could all share some time together.

Normally, we would go to Florida in the fall to get a shot of sunshine, but now, we had to overcome any hesitancy we might harbor after 9–11. Being married to a pilot, it was a rather moot question. We either would say "no" and be trapped by our fear, or say "yes" and step to the other side of our fears. We obviously said "yes".

While I felt a bit anxious, I was more determined to break through my concerns and share time with our son and his wife. When we made it to the ticket counter, a young soldier was standing next to his duffle bag, with a determined look on his face, as his vibrating knee betrayed his nervousness. The mother in me approached him to ask where he was going.

He said, "Iraq." And then quickly added, "I think we'll make short order of the mess, don't you, ma'am?"

"Yes, I agree," I said as if I were in some kind of authority over the matter. The truth is, no one knew for sure, but to every difficult question, there are two possible answers—either it will get better, or it will get worse. One of them will prove to be right. I choose to be an optimist. Optimists don't worry as much. That doesn't mean we don't worry at all, but we lean on a positive outcome, and that automatically reduces the negatives.

We chatted for a while, and then he heard his flight called.

"I have to leave now. Thank you, ma'am."

I waved goodbye as I said a silent prayer for his safe return.

Now, it was our turn. We boarded our flight and winged our way to Florida. The flight was wide-open, and the weather was perfect as we landed in Orlando. Sabrina had found a restaurant that had an equestrian show connected to it. I had been to dinner-theater before, but never with performing horses.

We sat down at tables that surrounded a dirt arena. After we finished our meal, the show began. Horses performed to music as they pranced, danced, and bowed in unison. The costuming and music were very enjoyable. Then came the grand finale.

The entire troop came strutting out on the stage decorated in red, white, and blue. They carried the American flag as they played several patriotic tunes. The audience burst into applause. When they played God Bless America, everyone, even seniors with canes and walkers, stood up. Old and young veterans stood at attention and saluted our flag as the national anthem was played. Patriotism blossomed out of thin air. The fear of our liberty being threatened seemed to bring us together.

When we returned home, we felt more determined, stronger, and hopeful. The only thing that had changed was our minds. We had a new view of the future—one of overcoming and not being defeated, either as an individual or a nation.

All over America, people were displaying our flag. Others, all the way to the west coast, were giving money and blood to those who were injured in the attack on the east coast. It was a wake-up call to think outside of ourselves.

Living beyond our fears was becoming a way of life, at least for those who chose to live that way. There were so many wonderful things to learn about ourselves on the other side of fear.

Terrorism hasn't gone away, but the way we define it in our minds will determine how much it controls us. If all the stories I've told so far, ring true for you, then begin to put your fears behind you and develop hope.

Do what you can, if you can, to take care of yourself and your family, but in the end, you need to lean more on God, who can resolve issues that are way too big for you.

CHAPTER 12

Alzheimer's

My command is this: Love each other as I have
loved you. Greater love has no one than this,
that one lay down one's life for one's friends.

(John 15:12–13 NIV)

Yep, that's a picture of my mother in the early stages
of Alzheimer's, enjoying her second childhood at Disney World when she was eighty-six. While she was more
aware of her surroundings, at that time, she began to
lose more and more of her memory while remaining
very happy and thankful. I begin with this image to remind you that not everything about Alzheimer's is sad.

In fact, in most cases, the patient isn't as negatively affected as the caregiver.

Alzheimer's has become a forgetful disease that is on the rise in America. This is partly due to the fact that we are living longer. Even though it is not as long as the patriarchs of the Old Testament, it is still longer than most retirees of seventy or eighty years ago.

The reason businesses set sixty-five as the retirement age and Social Security kicks in at that magic number is because that was the average lifespan of a man in the 1940s. Even King David only lived to be seventy.

But today, the average life expectancy of a man is 77.8 years.[30] When Nelson signed up for life insurance in 2013, the company told him his life expectancy was 85. I guess stress today is shortening our life expectancy. I hope this book helps. And I can attest to the fact that there are a lot more men and women living to be 100 because I am living in a retirement community where several ninety-five and 100-year-olds are not only alive but active and contributing to the lives of others.

Unfortunately, as my husband and I learned when we represented the Alzheimer's Association at different functions, dementia can affect any age group. Alzheimer's is a form of dementia, and it is often difficult to di-

---

30 Elizabeth Arias, Betzaida Tejada-Vera, and Farida Ahmad, "Provisional Life Expectancy Estimates for January through June, 2020," *Vital Statistics Rapid Release*, Number 010, https://www.cdc.gov/nchs/products/index. htm.

agnose. Parkinson's and the aftermath of a concussion can also take on similar characteristics.

After my father died of a heart attack, my mother began to show signs of dementia. She was already eighty-three, so normal senior forgetfulness was to be expected. However, the nurse that checked on her in her independent-living apartment felt we should have her checked out by a doctor. That same nurse also recommended we place her in assisted living, where she would receive more nursing care and we could be sure she is getting her meds and hot meals.

Finding a doctor who can diagnose an Alzheimer's patient accurately can be challenging, especially since the patient doesn't want to be discovered. So, in the case of my mother, when asked what was happening in the news just a few months after 9–11, she thought for a moment and then said, with a cute smile, "There's always something going on, isn't there?" Everyone laughed, and the doctor dismissed it as normal aging.

We had to find a psychologist, who specialized in the effects of Alzheimer's and would go through a barrage of tests to see if any of her symptoms fit the disease. It was amazing how accurate her findings were. The doctor suggested that my mother should be started on Aricept, the drug of choice for an Alzheimer's patient at the time. Even though this doctor felt mom had advanced Alzheimer's, she still felt the drug could help prevent any further decline.

We were able to place her in the assisted living facility on her campus, and she began taking the new drug. Mom really enjoyed her assisted living apartment. My mother would take walks around the lake, go to the library, and talk with her friends over meals in the dining room.

Then, one day, she began to roam. Being the clever lady that she was, she roamed at night, past the nurses' station and made her way down a series of hallways to the nursing home, where she thought my father was still residing. He had died five years earlier. After that, she was moved into the nursing home section of the facility, where she could receive closer monitoring.

Mom could not leave the nursing home without a family member or friend coming to get her. She would call me Helen, which was her sister's name. She thought dad was still alive, in another facility. Mom didn't remember any trips we took with her. She lived in one room with one bed, one dresser, and one chair with an adjoining bathroom.

Now, before you shed a tear for her or me and feel that it was really hard for me to see her decline and know that my mother had forgotten my name... remember who we're discussing. This wasn't about me. This was about my mother. And she wasn't upset about the size of her room. In her own words, "This is all I need." In the words of the staff and many of the friends she made, "It is time for her to be cared for more fully."

I wrote a book about my journey with my mother through Alzheimer's, titled, *Inside Mom's Mind*. It brings out the fact that the ones who tend to feel the most pain are the loved ones who want to be remembered, who want to carry on a conversation, and remember family events together. When it doesn't happen, they feel their parent has already died, and they visit them less and less or, sadly, they stop visiting altogether.

I understand the pain. But you have to stand in their shoes or slippers for a time. They want to be loved. They want to see familiar faces, which they do recognize; they just don't always have the right name connected to them.

If the patient is your biological mother or father, there is the added fear that you may suffer the same fate. My grandmother and two aunts had Alzheimer's. That's supposed to increase my chances of getting it, too, since I'm already seventy-nine. So, should I stop writing this book and begin to design my tombstone? Hardly.

There is so much that I learned from all of these trials. My purpose right now is to record those lessons so that others may glean from them.

If there is one lesson to offer that may help you if your loved one develops Alzheimer's, it would be to go to the place they are, in their mind. In other words, don't pressure them to remember your name. Don't hound them about what year it is. If they want to blow bubbles or color in a coloring book, join them. And if they tell you the same thing over and over during your visit, try to listen and maybe gently draw their attention to what's going on outside their window. I found that Mom loved to watch the birds gathering at her bird feeder. I would play the *Sound of Music*, over and over again, on her DVD player.

While Alzheimer's slowly destroys the brain, it usually isn't the cause of their death. My mother would jaunt around her floor with a walker as if she were in a race. She wound up falling and breaking her hip. We could have had her restrained and kept in her bed, but that's like locking your child in his room so that he doesn't fall or encounter any problems in his life. That would be crueler than the pain of a fracture. With the help of Hospice and our continued visits, my mother didn't suffer, but she did eventually die of heart failure at ninety-one.

The best and worst thing about Alzheimer's is that the patient doesn't remember. My mother didn't remember the hospital's difficulty in giving her an internal exam for a stomach ulcer or being x-rayed when she fractured her hip, but she also didn't remember the fireworks we took her to on the 4th of July.

She was always happy. She enjoyed everyone who came into her room, from family to nurses. She outlived her mother by seven years, she felt God was good to her, and she had everything she needed.

What more could anyone want?

CHAPTER 13

Loss of Your Spouse

Blessed are those who mourn; for they will be comforted.

(Matthew 5:4 NIV)

I could have said, "Loss of a loved one," but I chose "spouse" in the chapter title because it normally refers to the one closest to your heart. The one that knows your good and bad habits and still remains your best friend.

Now, I know that isn't always the case. I've run into enough widows who were either divorced or unhappily married. Presuming you had a reasonably good marriage for more than ten years, then the fear of losing your spouse is very high on your concern meter.

The degree of panic over the loss of a spouse depends on other factors, too, like how old are you? Do you have children still living at home? Are you in need of physical care from your spouse? Well, as you see, each widow or widower will experience different feelings over the loss of their partner.

Nelson and I were married fifty-three years. The beginning of our marriage was a bit stressful, as I imagine is true for many newlyweds. Since we hadn't had any children, we both worked for our first year. I, as a teacher, and Nelson as an airline pilot, which took him away from home for three to four days at a time. I would leave love notes in his luggage, and he would leave love notes behind cupboard doors. It was kind of romantic, but not the same as being together.

By our second year of marriage, we had our first child. I decided to be a stay-at-home mom, while Nelson continued to be the breadwinner. That seemed like a very traditional family, but it was difficult to work with only one car, to listen to a colicky baby cry day and night, and not have Nelson there for part of the week to share the workload and talk to me, when I was exhausted.

After our second child was born, we moved out to the country. City-slickers, though we were at the time, there were a lot of wonderful moments we shared together on our eight-acre mini-farm. I can still see the four of us, standing knee-deep in snow, watching three deer silently leaping through the woods on the other side of our creek. I remember listening to the sound of the owl in our woods at night and watching a deer rooting through the dried leaves, hunting for fallen apples, just outside our bay window.

There were a lot of challenges, too. We had to depend on a well for our water and a woodburning stove for our heat. Looking back on those times, the things that I felt were overwhelming seem rather insignificant now because of all the higher mountains we had yet to climb together as our anniversaries multiplied.

That's one of my points. Maybe you've only climbed one or two of those mountains, and the thought of losing a child or husband is just too awful to even contemplate. That's fine. God understands. God promises, in 1 Corinthians 10:13, that He will not suffer you to bear what He feels you are not able to. I paraphrased the verse, but that's basically its meaning. You may never go through what I have, or you may have gone through more than what I have.

I'm trying to assure you that God will be there for you. Just keep up communications with Him. Don't just text your thoughts, but sit down and talk them out with Him.

Mother Teresa was once quoted to say, "I know God will not give me anything I can't handle. I just wish that He didn't trust me **so** much."[31]

That's good advice for all of us. Rather than sitting around worrying about tomorrow, roll up your sleeves and see if you can help change today, or ask God to change your mind about tomorrow.

Several times, we begin to write a new chapter in our book. Our book is uniquely ours. Just like fingerprints are unique to each of us, so are our marriages.

As I said earlier, for as much as I missed our daughter, I was extremely glad that I had my husband and our son. Nelson was stable, loving, kind, and a hard worker. God's Holy Spirit was the glue that kept us together. Each mountain we climbed made us stronger and bonded us closer.

I thank the Lord that He kept us together. We didn't let the little foxes, the pesky smaller issues, divide us. It's funny how we can often get closer to our spouse during a real trial and then get picky and irritated because of some minor annoyance, like leaving a toilet seat up or nylons hanging over the shower door.

The Bible says it this way in the Song of Solomon 2:15 (MSG), "Then you must protect me from the foxes, foxes on the prowl, foxes who would like nothing bet-

---

31 "Quote by Mother Teresa," Quotes.Net. STANDS4 LLC, 2022, https://www.quotes.net/quote/4414.

ter than to get into our flowering garden." It's pointing out to a young couple, who are in love, that there are little things, bad choices and such that can destroy your growing love for each other. You need to protect your relationship from those little foxes.

We had moved into a double-wide modular home, basically a large trailer. It sat on a wooded lot in northwestern Pennsylvania. The trailer was constructed in the south and was not built to handle three feet of heavy snow that could pile up in one weekend.

So, one day, after a heavy snow began to melt, we discovered a large leak in our roof. It was wetting the ceiling material in our bedroom until the tiles began to sag. Afraid that the ceiling would completely collapse before we could address the leak, we began frantically to stack up the furniture to push against the wet tiles. It began to look like a Dr. Seuss cartoon, and that made me laugh. We both started laughing as we stopped to survey our problem. As awful as it was in that moment, it really was a *little fox*, compared to all the problems in this world.

Once our well was hit by lightning, and we didn't have water for a few days. We couldn't bathe, wash dishes, or even flush our toilets. That was a serious problem. As we gathered an array of receptacles to contain the water from an open spring down the road from us, we began to laugh and be thankful we had other options. That seeming disaster turned out to be a bonding experience for us that we relegated to a *little fox* that disrupts our daily routines.

Another time, some cows broke loose from a farm down the road and were headed for our front door. Neither of us had been raised on a farm or worked with a herd of cows, so the incident looked threatening to us. I mean, if those cows pushed over the fence on their farm, couldn't they do some serious damage to our modest mobile home?

Nelson went out to meet the challenge by just speaking calmly to the animals and prodding them with a stick to reverse their direction and head back to the road. I had to laugh as I watched my husband become a sort of pied piper of Dingman Road as he walked them back to their farm. Again, what could have been a catastrophe, turned out to be another *little fox* in our marriage.

After Kim's death, nothing seemed to reach that level of sadness again. Things got bad, but they eventually got better, and, yes, things that were going well would sometimes break down.

There's a kid's show called *Cowboy Dan*. One of his songs goes, "Life is for learning and learning for life."[32] It's simple, and it's true. As long as God gives us life, we

---

32 "Life Is for Learning by Cowboy Dan, Written by Dan Harrell, 2003," YouTube, Accessed March 11, 2022, https://www.youtube.com/watch?v=STsBhRMmZhM.

need to live it by learning new things and not just grumbling every day about things that went wrong.

After homeschooling and retirement, Nelson and I stepped out, yet again, on a new adventure. We began to entertain children with performances that included puppets and music. How many pilots would consider becoming a puppeteer or, for that matter, work with their wife? But Nelson did, and, what's more, he enjoyed it. He played Mr. Noah with the confidence of a veteran actor.

One time, when we were playing Mr. and Mrs. Noah for a church group of children, we began our act in the usual way. We came out singing *Arkie, Arkie* with me holding a real-looking chimpanzee puppet, and Nelson greeting the children with a lifelike fox puppet. We walked through the audience and then went up on the stage, in front of a backdrop.

I began with my lines, "My, I wonder what year this is? Can anyone tell me what year this is?"

One child answered, "1995."

To which I said, directing it to my husband, "Dear, did you hear that? This is 1995."

He was supposed to reply, "Wow! That's amazing."

As I turned to him to hear his reply, I found he had rested his head on his shepherd's staff and was snoring. I was stunned for a moment. We had rehearsed this over and over again. He knew his lines, and he was messing up my response. He enjoyed doing little things like that from time to time. Fortunately, I didn't blow it by either scolding him on the spot or getting flustered. I simply came up with an adlib that went, "Poor Noah is getting very old and hard of hearing. We'll have to wake him up. Let's all shout, 'Noah, wake up!'"

They did, he did, and we kept that little snoring bit in our future performances.

Did I ever get upset with Nelson or disappointed with him during all those years? Absolutely. Of course. Did I disappoint him or get him upset? Sure. He didn't show it, but I knew.

The point isn't that we had a perfect marriage but that we were able to get to the other side of our fears, differences, and problems. That's love, and that's what we had.

Then, in 2019, we made the **big** move. I was seventy-six, and Nelson was seventy-nine. We decided it was time to move into a retirement community rather than owning a house in a development. I wasn't getting around very well and needed a cane or, for long distances, a motorized wheelchair. We found a scooter that could fold up and go in the back of our car so that I could get around the zoo with our great-grandchildren.

With high blood pressure, gout, and being a bit overweight, I figured I would be the first to go. After all, Nelson was not on any medications, he would walk two miles every day, and he could still climb ladders and do yard work. The retirement community allowed him to have lots of places to walk, even hike, and golf, and I would have access to arts and crafts materials, which I enjoyed very much.

Then, just four months after moving in, the COVID Pandemic hit hard in March of 2020. Lots of the normal activities, like concerts and birthday parties, had to be canceled. It was inconvenient but not the end of our world.

We thought up ways to lighten the atmosphere for some of the residents. Nelson helped me put together a stuffed six-foot manikin that I dressed in clothes from Walmart. We named him Elmer and set him out in different places, once a week, throughout our three-story building. Elmer hid candy for the residents to find. Everyone, including the workers, loved Elmer. One woman stopped to talk to him every day.

Then, without warning, our lives took a dramatic turn for the worse. One afternoon in May, Nelson began to throw up blood and filled the commode with black stools. I was shocked. He was never sick. This couldn't be happening. He was rushed to the hospital in an ambulance, and, to make the situation even more difficult, he wasn't allowed to have any visitors.

After the ambulance pulled away, I sat on the edge of my bed and sobbed so hard that I didn't think it would stop. It was reminiscent of the mourning I had experienced in our daughter Kimberly's room after her death.

The hospital discovered he had a bleeding ulcer from the aspirin he took. That didn't sound so bad. We threw out the aspirin and began to design a new diet that would resolve his problem for good. But Nelson still wasn't able to hold down much food. He was losing weight rapidly. This was a man who hadn't fluctuated in his weight more than five pounds, since we were married, and now his ribs were showing, and he was looking gaunt.

He had some lumps on his face that were partly covered by his beard. The doctor wasn't concerned about them a month earlier but did add that we should keep an eye on them in case they changed any. Just one month after his diagnosis of a bleeding ulcer, those lumps began to get red and grew bigger every day. They didn't hurt, but they were sensitive.

The dermatologist found it to be a rare cancer that would require a specialist. After another month of trying to get a proper diagnosis for treatment, the Merkel cell cancer had taken over his entire body.

It was at that point that I met a man I never really knew before. My husband wasn't very vocal about his feelings, and he often thought along a more pessimistic path. His pictures on his passport and driver's license resembled an older, reserved man with a pensive look on his face. It's why he needed me. I would often get him out of his melancholy outlook.

But now, with me, ten miles away, in our new apartment, waiting for a ride to the hospital, I felt frustrated that I couldn't be there, around the clock, to comfort and encourage him and try to bring some laughter into his day.

When I entered his room, Nelson had just received the news that radiation treatment could only extend his life a few months but not cure the cancer. Fortunately, this hospital allowed visitors in his room, and we could touch as well as take off our masks during our visit.

We hugged, and then we talked. To my surprise, he had already signed the paperwork with a Hospice nurse, who was going to start treatment immediately. They were going to remove his IV, which was nourishing him, and allow him to, as he put it, "starve to death."

Tears filled my eyes as I thought of how hard that decision had to be. He said that he asked about how painful starving would be, and the nurse assured him that Hospice would take care of any discomfort he might have.

He told me he loved me, and he wanted to be sure that I would take care of myself. In fact, he was trying to arrange for a masseuse, which our facility offered, to come to our apartment to give me a full massage, to relax me. I told him I would consider that later, but right now, I wanted to know what he needed.

Nelson wanted to know that Kirk was giving me help. I said he was and that he was coming up to see him the next day.

With each visitor, Nelson smiled and was able to say something funny. My somber sweetheart managed to smile. Visitor after visitor came, and Nelson continued to talk and smile as his body grew weaker. One of our longtime friends, Bill and Carol Deets from Pennsylvania, was able to visit Nelson in his hospital room. Being a retired pastor, Bill administered communion to the four of us with grape juice and soda crackers. Nelson and I shared communion together on the Sunday morning, just hours before we were married, and now, fifty-three years later, we shared our last communion together until we would meet again, in a better place, under better circumstances.

In the last few days of his life, he was moved to the nursing home, just walking distance from our apartment. The problem was no visitors were allowed in, not even me, but I could visit through the window and blow kisses. We used our walkie-talkies to hear each other better.

He asked the nurse to set him up in front of the window, so he could see the faces of the visitors and me that came. Each time, he blew me a kiss and whispered, "I love you."

After a few days in the nursing home, I was finally allowed to meet him in the garden. I was told I had to remain at the far side of a long table. Nelson was wheeled in and sat at the other end. I wasn't allowed to touch him, so I blew him a kiss, and he gave me a faint smile as he lip-synched an "I love you" in the air.

He was too weak to talk, so I played a CD that we both enjoyed by the Booth Brothers. I sang, and he reached his one arm into the air for a brief moment as if to acknowledge God in heaven. Then the social worker, who brought him outside and had remained near him, said, "I'm sorry, but your husband needs to return to his room." She wasn't being cold, in fact, she had tears in her eyes, but he was very, very weak.

Later that same day, I got a call from the nurse on his floor to come over as soon as possible. I raced over there in my scooter/wheelchair. They allowed me to come in as long as I wore a mask and goggles.

Nelson was flat on his back with an oxygen mask on his face. He was breathing very slowly. The nurses had set out water, coffee, cookies, and such for me, while I kept vigil during the last moments of his life. I was allowed to remove my mask and goggles, but he wasn't able to see me. He couldn't even talk.

There was no time to grieve. I needed to respond with encouraging, loving words, not tears. I played the music I had left in his room as I sang and kept repeating, "I love you, dear, and we will be together soon. It's okay. You can leave. I'll be fine. We'll meet again. I promise..." I rubbed his hand and chest.

Then, he took a deep breath and exhaled, followed by silence. I turned to the nurse. She said, "Yes, he just died." I didn't cry. I had cried over all the doctor's decisions, but at that moment, I didn't cry. I felt relieved for him that all that pain and suffering had finally ended. I stayed long enough to say a last goodbye, and then I kissed him on the forehead... and I left.

As I exited the nursing home, the sun was just setting over our lake. Nelson and I loved to sit out on the decking and look over the lake with the fountain and the geese bobbing on the ripples. But this night was something very special. The sunset was unusually beautiful. It glowed in varying shades of orange and red. I sat alone in my wheelchair next to the lake and spoke to God.

I felt God had sent this sunset just for me. It was a promise that Nelson was no longer hurting and that God was welcoming him home. It gave me a peace, a feeling that made me want to sing. I was smiling. I couldn't believe it. I didn't know how to tell my friends why I felt so happy and peaceful at such an awful moment. It was a time when most widows would be crying and begging God to tell them why.

Beyond the fears and suffering, I was never so proud of my husband as I was about how he handled the most difficult decision of his life. He took charge, had peace, and even found humor at a very fearful time, seeing the end of his life just a matter of days away.

I had always been proud of his career, honesty, appearance, integrity, faithfulness, and his parenting... but he finished his race as well or better than any of those attributes. And it's interesting that of all the sports he had participated in, he was proudest of his racing achievements. He finished his last race with a strong faith in God's promises.

I just want to emphasize the fact that my experience of becoming a widow is uniquely mine. Don't compare your feelings with mine. I happened to feel happy and at peace right away. It may take longer for you, but I know you will come to that same response eventually as you continue to seek God's love.

As I said earlier, there are so many factors in how we react to the loss of a spouse, but one thing is for sure, build a relationship together, as a couple, with God at the center. Without the promise of the resurrection and eternity, the loss of anyone would be unbearable. If ever God needs to be the main focus in your life, it is when you are on the precipice between life and death.

CHAPTER 14

Being Alone

"...and lo, I am with you always, even to the end of the age."

(Matthew 28:20 NKJV)

Some people choose to be alone. I like being alone for a while. It allows me to have time to think and even be productive. But man was not meant to be alone for a long time. You might feel that a pet can substitute for a human relationship, but it doesn't. Pets are comforting but no substitute for a good friend or a life partner. And if, like my husband and I, you spent the better part of your life with, what many like to call, their *soul-mate*... and now they are gone... you feel alone, like never before.

As a child may say, after the death of a pet, "Does dead mean I'll never see them again?" and you reluctantly have to say, "That's right, you'll never see them again." But with the death of a loved one, the wonderful truth is that you will see them again, but not in this lifetime.

That may not seem very comforting if you are a young widow with little children to take care of and worrying about how you will pay all your bills, but as a nearly eighty-year-old widow, who figures she has about five more decent years left in her, the loss is more acceptable, even expected.

Kim's untimely death, at five years of age, now that was unexpected. I didn't really feel alone then because I had the duties of a wife and mother to fulfill. But when you're in the autumn of your life, you anticipate or *should* anticipate, that one of you will outlive the other. You should prepare all those end-of-life important papers.

Anyone who lost a loved one during the Pandemic suffered an even greater loneliness. In my case, we couldn't have a funeral or even a memorial service because it would gather too many people together in one small area. Masks would be required, and social distancing was also necessary. Churches were even closed.

I spent days making a large tri-fold poster that depicted my husband's life with wording that expressed who he was and how I felt. I was granted permission to display it in our lobby. Since we had only moved into the retirement community a year earlier, only a few individuals knew who we were. So, it helped a little to be able to give this tribute to my sweetheart.

When all the sympathy cards stopped coming and all the concerned friends went back to doing what they needed to do, and our son had to get back to his job, that's when I really felt the void. The emptiness. The aloneness.

That's also when I decided to become better acquainted with God and His Word.

Nelson and I had shared Bible studies, church services, and often prayed together, but when you are all alone, you aren't interrupted by anyone. You can talk out loud to God while you're cleaning up the kitchen, or you can begin to sing while you're making your bed, and that's just what I did.

I spoke to God out loud. I sang along with CDs of lively gospel music, like, "...the love of God swept over me, making me glad, making me glad..." or I'd just start singing happy tunes as I went about my work, such as "...Leave your worries on the doorstep. Just direct your feet to the sunny side of the street."

I would often look up at Nelson's picture on my wall above my work table and acknowledge things he said to me, like, "You were right, dear, I do watch too much TV.

But not so much anymore. I've found so many things to do."

Since I no longer had my husband to talk to or go shopping with, I began to look around for activities I could do with all my free time. While I had sold some handmade items at the Acorn Shop on our campus, the Pandemic closed the shop, so creating new inventory was on hold.

I continued to move Elmer from one floor to another and hide candy. As clever as I thought I was, the residents always found the chocolate treats, even when they were wedged in a crack of a cushion on the sofa.

Having started a book about our commercial flying experiences but not having had the time to finish it, with packing, moving, and caring for Nelson, I now had the time. My husband had already edited most of it, even helping me with the artwork, so it was a joy to see it to its completion. I called it *How to RELAX While Flying*. Each chapter was a delight to review as I read over our many adventures with a smile of contentment.

In fact, I would highly recommend that you journal your feelings and your pleasant memories as a kind of therapeutic activity. You may not publish it, but there is something very healing about expressing yourself.

Then, one day, as I glanced out my window to watch the first snowflakes of winter begin to swirl to the ground and blanket the area with a clean white cover, I took a closer look at the building just a few yards away from my apartment. It was the nursing home on our campus.

Months earlier, when the COVID Pandemic began, Nelson and I had watched an older gentleman park his car along the road and hobble over to the first-floor window of the nursing home on his walker. He tapped on the window, and we could see him smile as his lips moved. He was visiting his wife. He couldn't go inside to hold her hand or give her a kiss, but he was able to see her and visit through the glass partition.

As the weeks went by, that same scene was repeated again and again. After Nelson's stay in that same building, and the many other family members who had to visit through a glass wall, I began to see where my calling was. I needed to find a way to reach the patients with the one thing I had to share... hope and even joy. Oh, yes, and love. So, I found I had a lot more to share than I first thought if I could just find a way to get to those isolated souls.

Nelson and I had entertained in such places, in fact, in that very building twenty-five years earlier. We saw the joy and relief we could bring to some very lonely seniors, as well as the nurses who ministered to them. It made the nursing home a place of service for me. I wasn't a nurse. I don't even know that I could be a very good caregiver if I had to change diapers or clean their rooms, but I knew I could talk with them and cheer them up with the stickers and puppets we had collected.

"God," I began my little chat as I rummaged through my Rubbermaid storage container, "You put me just where you needed me, didn't you? Right across the street from my purpose." And with a grin, I continued, "Thank you, God, it's just what I needed."

I spent the cold days of winter finishing my book and putting together things that I could use to positively impact those isolated folk in the nursing home. I got a red wig to catch their eyes when I could have permission to go inside and entertain.

I used a red wig as a visiting clown twenty-five years earlier, and it really got the folks to sit up and smile. Now, I was one of the old folks in a wheelchair, so I really needed all the fun, youthful things I could find to perk up my audience.

When spring finally came, the nursing home was still closed, but many of the patients could come out on a warm day. It was unscheduled, so I took along some stickers and a few key chain characters to pass out to the random residents whenever I found them sitting in the sun in their wheelchairs.

While someone who has everything would probably find a sticker rather insignificant, these dear individuals giggled as they decided on which of the designs they wanted to stick on their wheelchairs. They thanked me, over and over, and I became known as *the sticker lady*.

Later, since I still wasn't allowed inside, I wrote a booklet filled with positive thoughts and colorful pictures, which the head of our community was willing to duplicate. With the help of a friend in my apartment complex, we stapled together over 200 booklets to be distributed to both the nursing home and assisted living residents.

Each day, God seemed to be flooding me with more and more ways to encourage all of the folks on our campus, and especially those who were not as mobile as the independent residents. My loneliness had disappeared. I still wear a mask, as it is required, for now, but I manage to communicate with positive words, cards, booklets, smiley stickers, and by humming a tune wherever I go.

Yes, I made the decision not to be depressed. I decided that a long time ago, even when I was just thirty-five, in my hospital bed, back in Meadville, Pennsylvania. But I couldn't produce joy to help me come out of my loneliness without God in the equation. He's the Creator of all the people and things that add joy to my life. That's like wanting to put a dollop of whipped cream on top of a slice of pumpkin pie, but you left out the pie. The Holy Spirit is the source of all the good stuff.

After nearly eight decades of living, I have concluded that there is no joy, no peace, and no love without God. And when I begin to dwell on the things I don't have, or when I feel forgotten or want to be pitied, I find that I am falling for the wiles of the Great Deceiver. Satan would love to distract me from my purpose and emphasize the negatives in my life.

That's when you have to turn on the music, start reading the scriptures and turn your attention to all the wonderful things you are thankful for. Remember past joys, be grateful for today, and be thankful for the promises of eternity. In fact, spend some time listing all the people, things, and experiences that you are thankful for because they all came from God. Yes, even that microwave, manufactured by Sunbeam, was inspired by God.

There is a book by Laura Hillenbrand and a movie titled: *Unbroken*. It is the true story of Louis Zamperini. It describes a young athlete, who ran in the 1936 Olympics in Berlin, and later joined the Army Air Force, serving as a bombardier on a B-24 Liberator in the South Pacific during WWII. [33]

His plane was shot down, and he drifted on a raft for twenty-seven days in Japanese-controlled waters until he was picked up by the Japanese and put in a prisoner of war camp. Louis was psychologically and physically brutalized and often left in solitary, cramped, and unsanitary cubicles, yet he managed to remain sane and

33 Laura Hillenbrand, 2014, Unbroken: A World War II Story of Survival, Resilience, and Redemption, Random House Trade Paperbacks; Reprint edition (July 29, 2014).

strong. His brother's words, "A moment of pain is worth a lifetime of glory," encouraged him when he was preparing for his running endurance, and it also helped to bolster his strength while he was in prison.[34] After the war, Louis had some adjusting to do, but over time, he realized that he had to find forgiveness for his tormentors. That's when he became a Christian evangelist.

He found, what I found, but in very different circumstances. Making the decision to change your thinking, finding a purpose, and then trying to help others through the lessons you learned from life, takes away your loneliness, anger, and frustration. It helps you begin a whole new chapter in your life, often better than the first half.

---

34 Ibid.

CHAPTER 15

COVID Pandemic

Peace I leave with you; my peace I give you.
I do not give to you as the world gives. Do
not let your hearts be troubled and do not be
afraid.

(John 14:27 NIV)

In March of 2020, our country was hit with a totally
unexpected bombshell. It seemed that some kind of
new virus from China, given the name, COVID-19, had
entered our country. While it had actually presented itself a few months earlier, no one seemed to think that
it was going to be much more of a problem than a new

strain of the flu. As the number of cases increased, more and more were hospitalized, and many died, we began to sit up and take notice.

Senior citizens seemed to be the most vulnerable to this virus. Nelson and I had just moved into our retirement community in October of 2019. The CDC was recommending face masks, but no one knew where to look for them or just what kind of mask was needed.

Several of the residents, including myself, had sewing machines. Jo Ann Fabrics was giving out free patterns, so their customers could create masks from various materials, along with some elastic to go over the ears.

There was a debate over which fabric was best, cotton or a less breathable material, such as polyester. In the end, we decided any mask was better than none, so we began to manufacture masks for our residents and our workers. There was such a demand for these materials by homemakers that Walmart and Jo Ann's were running out of fabrics.

And because of the uncertainty of how contagious this virus was, both establishments were limiting the number of customers that could enter their stores at one time. I remember seeing a long line of ladies standing outside of Jo Ann Fabrics, waiting to be allowed in, after one customer exited.

Stickers sprang up on the floors of every business establishment, advocating six feet of social distancing between customers. I even had a lady who worked the registers at Walmart offer me a mask she had made for any customers who inquired about masks. Some, like our son, chose to tie a cowboy bandana around his neck and pull it up whenever he was around people.

As the virus spread and we could see that it wasn't any ordinary flu, manufacturers started producing simple masks from lightweight materials. Group activities began to shut down on our campus, and the residents were feeling anxious and a bit irritated that so many events they had once enjoyed, like a concert or a card party, were no longer allowed. At one point, our entire campus was in lockdown. No one, not even local friends or family, was allowed in. Any deliveries were stopped at our two entrance gates and delivered by our workers. Only residents could come and go by showing their ID.

Nelson and I had seen the fear factor that was growing in our building and the community around us. While we were donning our masks and trying to keep the new social distancing recommendations, somehow, the fear and worry that was rising in others seemed bigger than any we had experienced. That's when Nelson and I constructed our silent, six-foot, completely sanitized manikin, Elmer, to be made available to our residents. He just sat quietly in a chair, allowing a person to sit next to him and even talk to him without the worry of contracting COVID.

With the addition of hiding a few pieces of candy around the building, it helped reduce the tension. Smiles were popping up, and conversations began to change from, "How will we survive this virus?" to "I found a Hershey bar in the flower pot on the second floor."

The real problem of this thing we called a pandemic was the confusion and anger that it had birthed. When we first learned of the virus, President Trump ordered the medical researchers to come up with a vaccine in what he called *Operation Warp Speed*. As the new vaccines rolled out, he was one of the first to receive it. But then we started getting mixed messages, like, don't get vaccinated because it hasn't been thoroughly tested. Don't trust science, and don't wear masks because it's unhealthy. Or how about the one that many Christians believed, which is that God will take care of you, so you don't need doctors.

Once President Biden took office, he increased the production and distribution of the vaccine, but the people were afraid to take it because of what they'd been told. So, the virus continued to spread, mutate and be a real threat to mostly unvaccinated people while the lifesaving vaccines sat in refrigeration, waiting to be used.

Fear had created frustration and worry. Worry for our own health, the health of our families, and the concern that the wearing of masks and social distancing will be the new norm.

In my retirement community of approximately 500 residents, we live in independent living villas and apartments, assisted living, or our nursing home on campus. Almost everyone has been vaccinated and had their booster shots. Those who work here, for the most part, have been vaccinated and are still tested twice every week.

Since receiving the vaccine, continuing to wear masks in public and to social distance, no one in our apartment complex has been hospitalized, although a few have had to quarantine for a few days because they did contract a mild case of the virus from somewhere.

The few that have had to be quarantined are those who have been out into public places. So, since no one in our Lakeshore Apartments has had COVID, and because most of us don't drive or drive very sparingly, one can assume that our wellness record can be attributed to our following the CDC's rules. They seem to be working, and, I might add, we have a large number of retired ministers in our community who are abiding by those rules, also. I'm not trying to play politics here, but politics and the media are interfering with the health and unity of our communities.

When I was in my thirties, I didn't like the fact that shots and pills were given out so quickly for every little ailment, but in this case, I am completely compliant. I owe it to my friends, here, at my retirement facility. We move in rather tight circles, interacting with each other and the workers here on a daily basis. I don't want to give any of them the virus that may be dormant in me, and I don't want them passing any viruses on to me. The vaccines are a win-win.

Over fifty years ago, all of America was lining up for the Polio vaccine. There were no debates in the government or the church. We did it to stay safe and to help others to be safe. We saw children with leg braces or having to spend their youth in an iron lung as a result of the disease. We were unified in our effort to stop it.

I just saw an unbelievable interview with a woman hooked up to a respirator in ICU who wasn't vaccinated and contracted COVID twice. When asked if she would finally get the vaccine, she said, in a weak voice, "No, I don't want to be vaccinated." She wanted all the nurses to serve her and save her life and expose themselves to the deadly virus, but she refused the vaccine.

Even before the polio shot was created, I was vaccinated for smallpox. You may say, "But we never hear of smallpox or polio today, so why get the vaccines?" You are answering your own question. You don't hear of those diseases because we vaccinated everyone.

I know you will probably add, "If God is protecting us, we don't need any medical assistance to stay healthy." As I mentioned, in regard to our daughter's death, I never thought our children would be seriously ill, let alone die. We Christians think we are in some kind of protective bubble. We're not. God helps us to have the strength to make it through our trials, but He is not going to protect us from everything. Trials are a part of a Christian's walk because we are a part of the human race, but the way we handle those trials is our witness to God's love.

Can God heal? Yes. Does He heal? Yes. Are there times He doesn't heal? Yes. Does He hate doctors? No. Luke was a doctor.

Fear is the biggest problem we have produced today: fear of the virus, fear of the doctors, fear of public places, fear of the vaccines, and a fear of just about everyone and everything around us. Violence and depression are born out of fear instead of love for our neighbor.

I have found that many residents in our building think that because nearly everyone is vaccinated and we all seem to be reasonably healthy, we don't need to worry about masks or social distancing. After two years of this virus, we are all a bit tired of the threat. We're tired of adding a mask to our fashion statement or breathing through four or five layers of materials. We want to get together, unmasked, with our friends and family. Believe me, I understand. And I do visit with my vaccinated family and friends, in my apartment, without masks. But in a large group, I wear it for their safety and for mine.

Quite a few seniors here have stopped watching the news. I can understand that, too. But if we aren't informed, how can we make a sensible decision? Even Jesus asked us to watch the fig tree. That was an admonition for us to pay attention to what is going on around us. You certainly don't have to watch 24/7 news coverage, but at least stay informed by brief summaries of the news on your computer or the six o'clock news broadcast.

Parents have had marches outside of schools to protest against the wearing of masks. Really? Which is more harmful to the child, wearing a mask or seeing his angry parent threatening other parents and authorities? Most of the children have no problem with wearing masks. I have two great-grandchildren in school, and they have come up with some pretty creative masks. It's not a problem for them or for their health.

Let me go back a little farther in history.

The first inoculations were done by a Puritan minister, Cotton Mather, in 1721.[35] Boston was in the midst of a devastating outbreak of smallpox. The vaccine stopped the spread of the virus, just as our vaccines are doing today. In fact, George Washington, our founding father and Christian president of the United States of America, *mandated* that all his troops be inoculated against smallpox in 1777.[36] In those days, they didn't

35 Wikipedia Contributors, "1721 Boston Smallpox Outbreak," In Wikipedia, The Free Encyclopedia, 2022, https://en.wikipedia.org/wiki/1721_Boston_smallpox_outbreak.

36 "Smallpox, Inoculation, and the Revolutionary War," U.S. National Park Service, 2021, https://www.nps.gov/articles/000/smallpox-inoculation-revolutionary-war.htm.

use needles to give inoculations; they slashed the flesh of the patient and physically smeared the pox into the open wound.

Aren't you glad we aren't living back then?

I like to be informed, whether it's about the weather or my health, for better or for worse. That's when I can make the best decision on how to go forward. The Bible says the truth will set you free.[37] Even if you don't like the truth, when you see or hear it, you need to accept the truth. If there are fewer cases of COVID in people who take the vaccine, then maybe, just maybe, there is some truth in getting vaccinated.

If ever we need to practice the Golden Rule, to care about others, it's now.

---

37 John 8:32.

CHAPTER 16

Growing Old

Even to your old age and gray hairs I am he, I
am he who will sustain you. I have made you
and I will carry you; I will sustain you and I
will rescue you.

(Isaiah 46:4 NIV)

How many times have you heard a senior citizen say,
with a wry smile, "Don't ever grow old?" I realize that he
is just trying to gently tell you that he is having some
discomfort associated with old age, like arthritis. Nevertheless, it's a rather threatening thing to say since
everyone, even that very active giggly toddler *will* grow

old, and, yes, they probably will experience a variety of senior issues, from absentmindedness to wrinkly skin, from missing teeth to the need for a walker.

I guess the biggest tragedy of growing old is that it reminds you of your mortality. I certainly wasn't thinking much about dying when I was dating, when I had my first child or had my first job. But when you see the signs of old age showing up in your mirror and joints, you either try to ignore them or start worrying about them.

Living in a retirement community, I am surrounded by folks who are as old or older than I am. Most of them are still quite active and happy. Of course, being quite active is relevant to one's age. If you're seventy-five and still working in your garden, that's quite active. If you've made it to ninety and can still walk without a walker or cane, that's quite active.

Most of us remember the day we could work all day, without a nap, and sleep through the night, with, maybe, one trip to the bathroom. You may have won trophies for some physical sporting event or been the winner of a beauty contest. You want that again. I understand. Unfortunately, that's the downside of growing old. You may win a senior sporting event, but you aren't going to compete in the Olympics.

If that defeats you and makes you obsess over dying, then you will have a very depressing ending to your life.

I have found that growing old has so much living to do in that dash between the dates on the tombstone, even when you are in your eighties.

Shannon Alder once said, "Beauty is not who you are on the outside, it is the wisdom and time you gave away to save another struggling soul like you."[38]

I often quoted Robert Browning to my husband, which said, "Grow old along with me! The best is yet to be, the last of life, for which the first was made."[39] All those wonderful talents and knowledge and even physical belongings you have acquired over the years can now be put to good use.

While my family members didn't find my rock collection of much interest to them, I met a young girl, about eleven, at our garage sale who was totally enthralled with rocks and fossils. I sold my extensive collection to her for a fraction of its worth. She later came to our house with her grandparents to thank me with a homemade card she had created just for me. We hugged, and her smile told me that she would probably go on to become a petrologist or paleontologist, working with fossils and rocks for the rest of her life.

---

38 "Quote by Shannon L. Alder," Goodreads.com., 2022, https://www.goodreads.com/quotes/1266415-beauty-is-not-who-you-are-on-the-outside-it.

39 "Quote by Robert Browning," Goodreads.com., 2022, https://www.goodreads.com/quotes/71023-grow-old-along-with-me-the-best-is-yet-to.

Another young lady, who went on our nursing home outreach performances to sing and play her flute, is now a geriatric musical therapist.

The interests I had when I was younger has led others to a future that will bring them great satisfaction. Even though I may no longer be able to do it myself, I can still help to inspire others.

Did you ever read the rest of Browning's poem? "Our times are in his hand who saith, 'A whole I planned, youth shows but half; Trust God: See all, nor be afraid!'"[40]

Interesting. He poetically says to "not be afraid." Yes, as natural as growing old is, it also has a lot of fear connected to it, depending on what you choose to dwell on.

Yes, I am concerned about any future health problems. What will finally be the cause of my death? But I have prayed about it, and I trust that God will not test me beyond what I can bear.[41] Knowing that, I can put that fear aside and get back to the more rewarding and pleasant activities that have the potential to put a smile on someone's face.

No matter how many good things you may want to do while you are on this earth, the aging process will eventually tell you that you can't do them anymore. It's kind of God's way of saying, "I'm ready to take you to

---

40 "The Assurance of Salvation in 'Rabbi Ben Ezra,'" The Victorian Web, 2009, https://victorianweb.org/authors/rb/trujillo3.html.

41 1 Corinthians 10:13.

the next level." Isn't eternal life the gift of what lies on the other side of death for a believer? Isn't it when we will abound with energy and be able to accomplish even greater things than we had ever imagined in a more glorious surroundings than we have ever known?

In your youth, you may have felt like you could conquer anything singlehandedly. But old age reminds you that you need God every minute of every day. You no longer can climb those stairs without grabbing a railing or sitting in a chairlift. As you look back over your life, you also realize how many times God had stepped in to help you when you may not have recognized His fingerprint on your accomplishments. Yes, growing old is humbling. As James 4:6 says (NIV), "...God opposes the proud but shows favor to the humble." So, be grateful for the lessons you have learned from your gray hairs.

I am not able to walk very much due to the car accident, and due to the fact I love drawing and writing, which means I don't put exercise very high on my list of routines. That's a part of the reason I require a wheelchair for long distances.

But I can attest to the fact that many seniors in my facility are in their eighties and nineties, and they never use a wheelchair or walker. Exercise is very important to them. Will they live to be 200? No one in our century has achieved that, so, I'm guessing, no. But even if they lived to be 500-years-old, how does that compare to eternity?

Which begs the question as to what you want to achieve at the end of your life? Are you trying to stay well and active as your victory trophy, or are you trying to maintain your health, so you can achieve more with the talents you have been given?

Your health is important at any age, but you have a lot more to give, even in your nineties, than just staying alive.

When my parents were in this retirement facility, there was a woman who was ninety-one that loved to get into full *white face*, to entertain at the nursing home, as a clown. She had clowned in her younger days and realized that she could still perform. By the way, having used clown makeup myself, it tends to soften your skin and keep it from getting dry and wrinkled. So, there is an added bonus if you think you want to try clowning.

No matter what your age, smiling is the best facelift there is. I've found children will listen to a senior because they often have a strong relationship with their grandparents. Thus, seniors make great storytellers, which is an excellent medium for teaching morals and strong family ties. I'm only sorry that COVID has held me back from doing that. Kids love to get attention and listen to stories, and we seniors love to be around children as we tell our stories—what a great way to spend our free time.

My inevitable death doesn't overshadow my vision for my future. My trust in God frees me to do all that I have yet to accomplish. That trust keeps me from getting bogged down in despair. I realize that a new problem may create a new fear. As you have seen, I have fallen into many fearful situations, but I have learned that turning to God's Word and reminding myself of His promises will bring me back to hope and peace.

Leo Tolstoy was a Russian writer considered to be the greatest writer of all time, having written *War and Peace*, *Anna Karenna*, and other novels. He lived from 1828 to 1910. When he was in his fifties, he said, "Five years ago, however, my faith came to me. I believed in Jesus Christ, and my whole life underwent a sudden and drastic transformation. Life and death cease to be an evil and a fear. Instead of despair, I tasted joy and happiness that death could not take away."[42] After that, he wrote such books as *The Kingdom of God Within You* and *Resurrection*. He lived to be eighty-two and definitely wasn't focused on how quickly his arteries were hardening.

Tolstoy's conclusion that he no longer had a fear of living or dying is very reminiscent of Paul's statement in Philippians 1:22–23. Paul was in prison and ready to die or continue to live and serve Jesus' followers. Either way, he was content. This also echoes the words of my friend, who, upon having inoperable cancer, said, "If I live, it will be to the glory of God, and if I die, it will be to the glory of God."

---

42 "Quote by Leo Tolstoy," Goodreads.com., 2022, https://www.goodreads.com/work/quotes/2847065.

We need to be prepared for our golden years in our thinking and by filling out all those important end-of-life papers. We need to do what we can to stay healthy and purpose-driven. Accept what we can't change and believe the Word of God while trying to eliminate any negative thoughts from our minds as we focus on God's love and hope.

CHAPTER 17

Fear of God?

We love because he first loved us.

(1 John 4:19 NIV)

What thoughts run through your mind when you think of God? I'm not asking what you've been trained to say, like God is love or God is good. I'm asking what you think of immediately when you are asked, "Who is God?"

Do you think of an angry God, sitting on a throne of judgment, ready to cast you into a fiery hell if you don't do everything He wants? Do you think of God as filled with a pent-up vengeance for the wicked that He will pour out over them at the White Throne Judgment? When you pray for others, is it always to keep them out of hell?

When my eighty-year-old father was in the nursing home, realizing that death was imminent, he asked us to pray with him, as he asked for God's forgiveness. After the prayer, he looked at me and said, "Do you think God could ever forgive me?"

This was a man who had been an elder in his church, who read his Bible every day, and who had worked hard to provide for his family, and yet, without telling us what he needed to be forgiven of, he asked the question that many may be asking, "Can God forgive me?"

I assured him that He not only could, but He did. However, there was something more inherent in his question. Isn't it also revealing a deep-seated fear of God?

You may quote Proverbs 1:7 (NIV), "The fear of the Lord is the beginning of knowledge..." as your reason to be scared of God, but what does *the fear of the Lord* really mean?

If you are a parent, you should be able to understand this passage. You don't want your children to tremble or hide when you enter the room. That's not a good relationship to have with anyone.

God had wonderful friendly chit-chats with Adam and Eve in the Garden of Eden before Satan came into the picture. Adam and Eve enjoyed following God's instructions because God's teachings were good. It was good for the couple, good for the land, and it left everyone happy.

I'm sure you want your children to be happy, to share time with you, and not be afraid of you. So, the *fear* you want your children to have isn't to be frightened of you, but for them to respect what you say because they acknowledge your authority as a parent and they believe you, even if they never tested your words.

If you tell your child not to take drugs, even though they never tried them, you want them to believe you and obey you. If they obey you, they remain happy—making good grades, and staying out of trouble. So, your teaching has been for their benefit.

If they don't listen to you, life will be their teacher, and they will have to learn the hard way that you were right. You don't stop loving them, but you sadly have to watch them hurt themselves through their disobedience. Nevertheless, out of their suffering, many prison ministries have proven to be a turning point for a wayward child or adult.

Kind of like Adam and Eve. When they felt equal with the Lord to the point of disrespecting His words... or in Biblical terms... they stopped *fearing the Lord*, they began to test God's teachings. They began to sin, and that's when God had to put them out of the garden and have them face the consequences of their disobedience. Did God stop loving them? No. He just wanted them to know what sin does to a person and to have them teach it to their children's children.

God hates sin but not the sinner. While there is no verse in the Bible that says, "we are to love the sinner but hate the sin," it is implied by many other verses that ask us to love our enemies and to forgive others. God represents a perfect love, which we are gradually learning to emulate. In God's mind, He is able to hate sin and still love the sinner. Not so much with us. We tend to hold on to our hurts and dislikes. And yet, the closer we get to God's agape love, the closer we are to the heart of God.

It's interesting that even the word hate has a different meaning in the Scriptures. In most cases, it means to love less, not despise, and wish someone were dead, as we might interpret the Word. So, when it says to "... hate your father and mother..." in Luke 14:26 (NIV), it is not asking you to despise your parents but to love them less than Jesus.

On the other hand, when the Bible refers to God hating sin, that takes on a different meaning. It *does* mean to *despise* sin. We need to totally hate any behavior or thought that separates us from God.

I was exposed to a rather diversified Christian upbringing. To begin with, my three grandparents came from very different backgrounds. My mother's mother was a widow. She and her husband immigrated to America in their teens from Austria, before WWI. They were Greek Catholic. They had twelve children. Three died young, and the remaining nine worked on the farm while my grandfather worked in the coal mines. When he died, the three oldest children had to find jobs to help support their family. My mother worked as a waitress and later as a maid at the age of fifteen. With only an eighth-grade education, she managed to pay her bills and send money home to her mother. Then, at twenty-four, she met my dad in the midst of the Great Depression, while working as a live-in-maid in Cleveland, Ohio.

My father's parents had been born in America and were casual Protestant church goers. My grandma's heritage was from Germany, and my grandpa could trace his roots back to the Isle of Man, a little island between Ireland and Scotland in the Irish Sea. They had two sons and lived in the suburbs of Cleveland, in the little town of Bedford. Grandpa worked as a machinist, and grandma was a nurse, working with the mentally ill. While she often showed my brother and me a good time at playgrounds, on picnics, and at amusement parks, she also introduced us to tarot cards, reading tea leaves, and the Ouija board.

My mother left the Catholic church when she started working in Pittsburgh with her sister, but she remained devoted to church attendance. My father, on the other hand, had learned about God and the Bible through his early Sunday School days but was not accustomed to regular adult church services.

When my brother and I came along, my parents both agreed that children should be taught about God in a church. The closest church to us, within walking distance and without crossing a street, was a very strict Baptist congregation that forbids any dancing, movie-going, or singing of any music, except their hymns.

Needless to say, since my parents didn't attend that church, they allowed us to go to the movies (most of which were innocent Disney films, like Bambi) and listen to popular music by Bing Crosby and Dinah Shore. I even took tap dancing lessons at the YMCA. As a child, it made things a bit confusing as to which rules to follow.

My mother had always made me say a prayer before I went to bed. And when dad was in the Army, she would put his picture in front of me and say, "Don't forget to pray for your father to come home safely."

I always remember my father reading his Bible just about every day, and he often prayed silently, standing in front of a window while touching his elbow. He was very strict about us not playing or doing any kind of work on the Sabbath, except for Mom, who made us wonderful meals. Dad didn't want to anger God, but he didn't attend church, except on special occasions... like Christmas and Easter.

When my brother was a teenager, he chose to go to a Congregational church. Once my parents attended with him, they found it to be a place where they felt comfortable. My father not only decided to attend as a family every Sunday but wanted us all to be baptized there. So, to my great surprise and delight, we all donned white robes and were baptized in the church baptismal tank, privately, after services.

I had been Christened in a Methodist church, raised in a Baptist church, and at the age of twelve, baptized into a Congregational church. When my father transferred to Pittsburgh, we lived near the Greater Pittsburgh Airport in Moon Township and attended a Presbyterian church. If all of that bouncing around did anything for me, it left me with the realization that no one church denomination had all the answers.

In spite of the many different church philosophies, I had concentrated on the love I was taught through the flannel board stories and the heart-warming hymns I sang in the choir. I especially enjoyed the Christmas season. Everyone, even atheists and Jews, gravitates to the joy, love, and generosity that is poured out during the Christmas season.

When Nelson and I married in the midst of the tumultuous '60s, we wanted to find a church that hadn't watered down God's Word nor was filled with fear or hatred for the nonbeliever. So, we joined a church that kept to the Word of God, from Genesis to Revelation. It was stabilizing at a time when morals seemed to be evaporating, but it, too, didn't emphasize the love of God as it should have. Since Nelson would often be gone for days due to his flights, we agreed to read one Bible chapter each day, so we would be on the same page when he returned from his trip.

Realizing that no church was perfect, we decided to add our own Bible study to our daily routine and develop a personal relationship with God that emphasized love, grace, and forgiveness.

No church can get you to heaven. That is a gift that God gives to those who believe in His Son. So, no matter what denomination you are associated with, you must learn from the Bible and all the trials and experiences that life dishes out to grow in Christ. You need to come to love God for who He is to you, personally, by reading His Word, talking to Him, and deciding to make the right choices.

When you fall short of the perfection you wanted to attain, remember, it is not your perfection that you should strive towards. Our perfection is in who Jesus is. It's your deep love and affection for Jesus and *His* righteousness that God sees in you. You are under His Grace, so you don't have to be worried all the time.

I used to steep burdens and guilt on myself. I would set the alarm to go off in an hour as I stayed on my knees, often finding my thoughts drifting to duties I had to do around the house. I felt that an hour's prayer at the start of my day was essential to my Christian walk. At the end of the day, I felt obligated to remember and repent of every sin I committed or even thought of in the last twenty-four hours, or I felt condemned.

Jesus said in Matthew 11:28–30 (NIV), "Come to me, all you who are weary and burdened, and I will give you rest (...) For my yoke is easy and my burden is light." Why is it, we seem to want to pay for a crime we have committed when we know Jesus has already paid for it? We keep feeling guilty for a sin we committed years ago, even though Jesus has taken away that sin. That's where I needed to take God's love to the next plateau.

I knew who Jesus was. I knew what He did by dying on the cross, but yet I kept feeling like I didn't deserve it, or I kept failing, and I couldn't forgive myself.

I had to come to the realization that Jesus didn't die just to forgive my sins, which He did, but to build a family bond with me—to make me a part of the God family, to share in my thoughts, and to help me to understand God's thoughts better. They aren't filled with anger or revenge. God is filled with love. God is Love.

Hard as that is to understand, think of a little toddler standing before his mother, who had told him not to eat the cookies before dinner. He shakes his head and says, "I didn't eat any cookies," as the crumbs on his cheeks betray him. Does the mother pounce on him and say, "You are lying!" or does she sit down, draw him near her, give him a hug and say, "Sweetheart, you need to tell the truth. I won't hate you. But I know you ate the cookies. So just tell the truth."

God wants me to recognize where I'm wrong. It's why He gave us the Ten Commandments, but He doesn't want us to be destroyed by them. As I worked within God's Way, I found myself filled with joy and peace that others can't understand, that doesn't even make sense to me. My guilt disappeared, and I experienced the freedom to be all that God had in mind for me to be.

Now, I pray without even thinking about it. I can't get on my knees anymore due to the injuries I incurred, so I often lean back in my recliner, and we just chat, God and me. Most of the time, I thank Him for all the things I see that He has done and is doing. I often feel I can hear Him laugh at some of the foolishness of we mortals. I ask His help with a project I'm on, like this book, and remind Him of certain persons I love and some who need to be loved. Realizing that God already knows my needs, I concentrate more on asking Him to open my eyes and heart to things I don't yet understand.

It may seem hard to find the time to chat with God, but doesn't anything worth having require some effort? Your career and your marriage require some work on your part to reach their full potential, so why wouldn't the most important part of your life, an eternal relationship with the Lord, be worth the effort?

Look around you, past the pollution, the bad news, and the paved miles of roads that *man* has made, to all the beauty and diversity God has made. This is a beauty that has endured the follies of man, the wars, the pollution, the greed. As Genesis 1:31 states, "it is *GOOD!*" It's why we need to see God through the eyes of a child.

Children don't concern themselves with politics or taxes or even wars; they are just interested in playing with their furry pets. They like to laugh and run and play in the open fields, picking flowers and watching an inchworm crawl slowly across a leaf.

We are so busy that we have forgotten how to laugh or be amazed. We forgot how to love, or we may never have learned what love is, let alone understand the unselfish kind of love that the Bible calls agape. That is the God kind of love that Jesus desires for us to develop.

When Nelson and I would take our great-grandchildren to the zoo, they would come bounding out the front door of their house shouting, "Gammy, Papak, I love you." They were filled with the anticipation of the fun they would have with us. They weren't told what to say or do. It was spontaneous.

That's the kind of vision we need to have of God. Thinking of Him should conjure up visions of joy and excitement... not fear. It's why Jesus enjoyed the giggling children who impulsively came running up to Him because they loved His stories and His gentle touch. The disciples were seeking peace and obedience, but Jesus was savoring the genuine love and joy of a child.

Yes, we need to have a Godly fear that helps us make the right choices for our joy now and for our eternal blessings later. Without genuine love, we are but *tinkling cymbals*, advocating love but dishing out judgments and anger. Christians should be filled with love, joy, and peace. We should have a song in our hearts and a smile on our faces, most of the time, not just for show but also behind closed doors. And even when things go wrong, especially when things go wrong, it develops our Christian character. With more love in our hearts, we will have more love and encouragement to give to others.

We need to have 1 Corinthians 13 made into a plaque to hang on our wall to be read every day before we go out the door.

CHAPTER 18

Let's Review

After all the stories, quotes, Bible verses, and lessons I've shared with you about how God worked with me through my fears, I thought it might be a good time to review some of the most important elements of each chapter.

Pray

Prayer is always a good place to start, but what we pray about is very important. Don't just recite a prayer. Let God know the desires of your heart. Open up to Him with your honest thoughts and feelings. He already knows everything about you, but He wants to hear you humble yourself and ask for His help. Prayer is not just for you to tell God what He needs to do but for you to listen and hear what He wants you to learn.

Be Teachable

If the Holy Spirit has nudged you to do something that you didn't want to do, maybe to change you and not the other person, will you do it? Changing our minds isn't easy. Especially when we become senior citizens, we tend to become set in our ways. But change is an important part of being a follower of God; even if you've celebrated your eightieth birthday, you can still acknowledge that God isn't finished with you yet. You still have a lot to learn.

Meditate on the Scriptures

I don't just mean to read one chapter each day. I did that when we were first married. It was much like having a reading assignment in school that was meant to help you obtain a good grade on a future test. Meditate on God's Word to allow yourself some quiet time to think. Think about the full meaning of the words you just read. Use a study Bible to help you understand the context of the verse. See how God's Word can help you in your daily life.

Count Your Blessings

It's not like you haven't heard that before. But are you able to count your blessings when everything seems to be going wrong? Joseph never walked away from God, and he never seemed to be bitter, even though he was sold into slavery and wrongfully imprisoned in Egypt. And yet, in prison, he became a model prisoner and later was made second in command under the Pharoah because he never felt abandoned by God. When Nelson died and I was all alone in our apartment, I thought my purpose had ended, but God showed up with a new plan for me in a new direction.

Be Thankful

If you are able to see the world around you, with or without glasses, give thanks to God. If you are able to hear, give Him even more thanks. Can you walk without assistance? Do you have a family? Friends? Do you live in a house or an apartment? Do you have enough food to eat? Do you have running water? Do you own a phone? A TV? The list goes on and on. So many things we take for granted that we should be thanking God for every day. Also, remember to be thankful to anyone who has helped you, from the checkout person at the grocery store to your husband heating up a can of soup for your lunch.

Serve Others

When we are toddlers, everyone seems to be serving us. If they didn't feed us, shelter us, and take care of us, we wouldn't be here. After we leave home, we often think that we are entitled—that everyone should still be serving us. But Jesus wants us to mature and learn to be servants. Wow! The King of Kings is the greatest servant of all, who wants us to learn to serve. Look around and see where you may be able to serve someone else. Give your time, money, or labor to bring back hope in their lives. And a real bonus is that serving others helps to take your mind off any fears you may have.

Encourage Others

It's one thing to serve others, but it's important to encourage them as well. A caregiver can comfort someone who is ill by changing the patient's bedding and giving them a back massage, but if that same caregiver can add kind and comforting words to their service, the patient will feel even better almost immediately.

Don't Believe Everything You Hear

In these end times, we are admonished not to be deceived with empty words and to discern the things we see and hear to be sure that they please the Lord.[43] Read and know what the Word of God is trying to teach you so that you can recognize the truth when you hear it and turn away from lies.

Journal

It's like keeping a diary or a log. The more honest you are in your journal, the more helpful it will be for you to see how you have grown or what you need to do. I encouraged my husband to keep a journal without know-

---

43 Ephesians 5-6.

ing he only had a year to live. He addressed it to our son to let him know the valuable lessons life had taught him. That journal has become a treasured gift to Kirk.

Find Your Purpose

Nothing can persuade you to crawl out of bed in the morning quicker than having a purpose. A godly purpose—one that includes helping others. If your mind is full of purpose, you don't have room for fear. Ask God what He wants you to do with your life. Then listen. Often, we find that we have been shown our purpose through the things people have said about us. "You're so good with children." "You always encourage me." "You work well with the elderly." "You have a way with words."

Be Generous

It's important to remember God first with our tithe. Ten percent given to God's work every month is just a guideline for being generous. As it says in Galatians 6:7 (NIV), "...A man reaps what he sows." It's a starting point for putting God first, and it's not just about money. Being generous with your time, listening to a worried friend, or visiting a shut-in, are also important.

It's Time to Laugh

The Bible shows us that there is a time for every feeling, including laughter. Laughter has been a remedy for many illnesses, and it's a way out of depression. Having a sense of humor can get you over a lot of hurdles in your life. Look for the humor in everyday things, such as finding that you put your cellphone in the refrigerator by mistake. Watch a funny movie or read a funny book, like one by Barbara Johnson. What we call humor today can be misleading, full of sarcasm and put-downs, so keep tuned in to God's guidance as you make your selections.

Look for Beauty and Wonder

Sex sells today and messes up our definition of just what beauty is. I'm talking about the beauty that is everywhere in God's creation—from the delicate buttercup, splashing a swath of yellow across an open field to the frisky squirrel, dashing from tree to tree, gathering his food supply for the cold winter ahead. We need to restore the beauty and wonder we had in our childhood when we first watched the gentle snowflakes blanket our world in white or stood awe-struck at a rainbow in the sky.

Stop Talking Negatively

Our words can build up or tear down. Our words affect others, but our words also affect us. How we think or talk can lead us into fear and depression. "Things will never get better" are the words that can destroy even the most optimistic person. That may also mean that you need to reduce your time spent with negative individuals. Just as we say, you are what you eat; it can also be said that you are what you think. So, see the glass as half full and not half empty.

Learn Patience

If you're stuck in traffic, long waits in a doctor's office, spending time in the hospital, or snowed in at home when you can't get to work, make that a special time to spend with God. Have a meditation book downloaded on your phone or have a book handy in your purse or glove compartment to not only distract you from the irritation of having to wait but to teach you *while* you wait.

Learn How to Relax And Enjoy

I've revived numerable old sayings, so let me quote one more. *All work and no play make Jack a dull boy.* With only chores and work ahead of us, it is hard to feel inspired, let alone inspire someone else. If you are a designated caregiver, you must give yourself the luxury to enjoy a delicious, quiet meal away from your workplace, take time to share a good movie with a friend, or just take a well-deserved nap in the middle of the afternoon, without any guilt. Even Jesus enjoyed three days at a wedding celebration before he began his demanding ministry.

References

"104 Mother Teresa Quotes on Giving & Kindness (LOVE)." 2022. Gracious Quotes. 2022. https://graciousquotes.com/mother-teresa/.

"115 Years Ago: Wright Brothers Make History at Kitty Hawk." 2021. National Aeronautics and Space Administration. 2021. https://www.nasa.gov/feature/115-years-ago-wright-brothers-make-history-at-kitty-hawk.

Arias, Elizabeth, Betzaida Tejada-Vera, and Farida Ahmad. 2021. "Provisional Life Expectancy Estimates for January through June, 2020." *Vital Statistics Rapid Release, Number 010.* https://www.cdc.gov/nchs/products/index.htm.

Dornhelm, Robert, Simon Wincer, Sergio Mimica-Gezzan, Michael w. Watkins, Timothy Van Patten, and Jeremy Podeswa. 2005. *Into the West - Part 2* (Manifest Destiny). YouTube. https://www.youtube.com/watch?v=GCnayRFj-2M.

"George Stephenson's First Steam Loco-motive." 2022. History Today. 2022. https://www.historytoday.com/archive/george-stephensons-first-steam-locomotive.

Handlebar. 2022. "'Beloved No. 1 Comedian' (Part 1): 'Just Homefolks.'" Hometown. 2022. https://hometownbyhandlebar.com/?p=31964.

Harwood, William. 2021. "William Shatner Sets Record in Space with Blue Origin Space-flight." CBS News Interactive Inc. 2021. https://www.cbsnews.com/live-updates/william-shatner-blue-origin-space-flight/.

Hillenbrand, Laura. 2014. *Unbroken : A World War II Story of Survival, Resilience, and Redemption*. Random House Trade Paperbacks; Reprint edition (July 29, 2014).

"Karl Benz." 2022. The American Society of Mechanical Engineers. 2022. https://www.asme.org/topics-resources/content/karl-benz.

"Life Is for Learning by Cowboy Dan, Written by Dan Harrell, 2003." n.d. YouTube. Accessed March 11, 2022. https://www.youtube.com/watch?v=STsBhRMmZhM.

Pleasance, Chris. 2020. "Russia Releases Never-before-Seen Footage of the Tsar Bomba Test." Daily Mail Online. 2020. https://www.dailymail.co.uk/news/article-8665553/Russia-releases-never-seen-footage-Tsar-Bomba-test.html.

Ponio, Judy. 2021. "How Mother Teresa Changed the World - Our Father's House Soup Kitchen." Our Father's House Soup Kitchen. 2021. https://ofhsoup-kitchen.org/mother-teresa-charity.

"Quote by Franklin D. Roosevelt." 2022. BrainyQuote. 2022. https://www.brainyquote.com/quotes/franklin_d_roosevelt_109480.

"Quote by Helen Keller." 2022. BrainyQuote. 2022. https://www.brainyquote.com/quotes/helen_keller_121787.

"Quote by Leo Tolstoy." 2022. Goodreads.Com. 2022. https://www.goodreads.com/work/quotes/2847065.

"Quote by Mother Teresa." 2022. Quotes.Net. STANDS4 LLC. 2022. https://www.quotes.net/quote/4414.

"Quote by Robert Browning." 2022. Goodreads.Com. 2022. https://www.goodreads.com/quotes/71023-grow-old-along-with-me-the-best-is-yet-to.

"Quote by Shannon L. Alder." 2022. Goodreads.Com. 2022. https://www.goodreads.com/quotes/1266415-beauty-is-not-who-you-are-on-the-outside-it.

"Quote by Socrates." 2022. BrainyQuote. 2022. https://www.brainyquote.com/quotes/socrates_163092.

"Quote by Zig Ziglar." 2022. Goodreads, Inc. 2022. https://www.goodreads.com/quotes/976049-f-e-a-r-has-two-meanings-forget-everything-and-run-or-face.

Rosenberg, Eric. 2021. "Fastest Airplanes Commercial Passengers Can Fly." NerdWallet. 2021. https://www.nerdwallet.com/article/travel/fastest-airplanes-commercial-passengers-can-fly.

"Smallpox, Inoculation, and the Revolutionary War." 2021. U.S. National Park Sevice. 2021. https://www.nps.gov/articles/000/smallpox-inoculation-revolutionary-war.htm.

"Sometimes He Calms the Storm Lyrics by the Ball Brothers." 2022. SongLyrics. 2022. https://www.songlyrics.com/the-ball-brothers/sometimes-he-calms-the-storm-lyrics/.

"The Assurance of Salvation in 'Rabbi Ben Ezra.'" 2009. The Victorian Web. 2009. https://victorianweb.org/authors/rb/trujillo3.html.

The Editors of Encyclopaedia Britannica. 2021. "John D. Rockefeller." In *Encyclopaedia Britannica*. https://www.britannica.com/biography/John-D-Rockefeller.

———. 2022. "Helen Keller." In *Encyclopaedia Britannica*. https://www.britannica.com/biography/Helen-Keller.

"Thomas Alva Edison." 2018. In *Development of the Industrial U.S. Reference Library*. *Encyclopedia.Com*. https://www.encyclopedia.com/people/science-and-technology/electrical-engineering-biographies/thomas-alva-edison.

Waterhouse, Benjamin. 2022. "Tech Giants: Steve Jobs and Bill Gates." Bill of Rights Institute. 2022. https://billofrightsinstitute.org/essays/tech-giants-steve-jobs-and-bill-gates.

Watkins, Elizabeth Siegel. 2012. "How Pill Became a Lifestyle Drug: The Pharmaceutical Industry and Birth Control in the United States since 1960." *American Journal of Public Health* 102 (8): 1462–72. https://doi.org/10.2105/AJPH.2012.300706.

Wikipedia Contributors. 2022a. "1721 Boston Smallpox Outbreak." In *Wikipedia, The Free Encyclopedia*. https://en.wikipedia.org/wiki/1721_Boston_smallpox_outbreak.

———. 2022b. "Cuban Missile Crisis." *Wikipedia, The Free Encyclopedia*. 2022. https://en.wikipedia.org/wiki/Cuban_Missile_Crisis.

———. 2022c. "Franklin D. Roosevelt." *Wikipedia, The Free Encyclopedia*. 2022. https://en.wikipedia.org/wiki/Franklin_D._Roosevelt.

———. 2022d. "Serenity Prayer." Wikipedia, *The Free Encyclopedia*. 2022. https://en.wikipedia.org/wiki/Serenity_Prayer.

"Will Smith and His First Skydiving Experience." 2022. SkyXtreme.Tv. 2022. https://skyxtreme.tv/what-skydiving-taught-me-about-fear-storytime/.

About the Author

Donna Trickett has had several diversified roles in her life, from daughter and wife to mother, grandmother, and great grandmother. Donna has enjoyed being a teacher, entrepreneur of several small businesses, working with her husband Nelson as a children's performer, and beginning their own outreach program to schools, churches, and nursing homes. Because Nelson took early retirement from the airline, they were both able to work together as caregivers to Donna's parents, speakers for the Alzheimer's Association of Ohio, as well as conduct workshops for caregivers.

At the age of sixty, Donna decided to take a correspondence writing course to prepare her to create the books that she had already written in her heart for so many years. That began her new journey as author and illustrator of five books: Treasures from the Wreckage, Inside Mom's Mind, Caregiving 101, How to RELAX While Flying, and Standing Strong Through Life's Storms

CPSIA information can be obtained
at www.ICGtesting.com
Printed in the USA
JSHW041457300622
27461JS00003B/10